FAST TRACK

to

SAILING

LEARN TO SAIL IN THREE DAYS

P9-DCJ-857

FAST TRACK

to

SAILING

LEARN TO SAIL IN THREE DAYS

Steve and Doris Colgate

INTERNATIONAL MARINE / McGRAW-HILL

Camden, Maine • New York • Chicago • San Francisco • Lisbon •
London • Madrid • Mexico City • Milan • New Delhi • San Juan • Seoul •
Singapore • Sydney • Toronto

The **McGraw·Hill** Companies

4 5 6 7 8 9 CTPS CTPS 1 9 8 7 6 5 4 3

© 2009 by Steve and Doris Colgate
All rights reserved. The publisher takes no responsibility for the use of any
of the materials or methods described in this book, nor for the products thereof.
The name "International Marine" and the International Marine logo
are trademarks of The McGraw-Hill Companies. Printed in China.

Library of Congress Cataloging-in-Publication Data
is available from the Library of Congress.
ISBN 978-0-07-161519-8
MHID 0-07-161519-9

Questions regarding the content
of this book should be addressed to
www.internationalmarine.com

Questions regarding the ordering
of this book should be addressed to
The McGraw-Hill Companies
Customer Service Department
P.O. Box 547
Blacklick, OH 43004
Retail customers: 1-800-262-4729
Bookstores: 1-800-722-4726

Photography supplied by the authors, Billy Black, Dana Bowden.
Illustrations by Affinity Design Group. Illustrations on pages 18 (middle), 37,
69 (bottom), 88 (top) by Elayne Sears. Illustration on page 75 by U.S. Coast Guard.

The Westport Library
Westport, Connecticut
203-291-4840

CONTENTS

DAY ONE

GETTING TO KNOW YOUR BOAT

CHAPTER 1

The Language of Sailing   4

CHAPTER 2

Start Sailing   13

CHAPTER 3

The Points of Sail   24

DAY TWO

BUILDING CONFIDENCE AND SKILLS

CHAPTER 4

Wind and Sails:
A Powerful Team   39

FOREWORD

As owner of The Moorings and Sunsail, the largest sailboat charter companies in the world, TUI Marine has 1,500 charter boats in service at forty-two bases in twenty-one countries. We are constantly on the lookout for capable sailors as clients. Steve and Doris Colgate, the owner/operators of the Offshore Sailing School, have developed more than 100,000 such sailors in their many years of teaching sailing. They have done so by never lowering their teaching standards and by perfecting a tried and true system that covers all the ways people learn: visual, auditory, and kinesthetic. First they send the aspiring sailor a book to study at home before the course (visual). This book, *Fast Track to Sailing,* is the culmination of years of development through their introductory sailing program. Second, one of their excellent licensed and certified instructors explains sailing in a series of classroom sessions to reinforce the book (auditory). Third and most important, the new sailor sets sail for comprehensive sessions on the Colgate 26 sailboat, which was designed by Steve specifically for sail training (kinesthetic). At the end of the course, the participant sails without an instructor, gaining the confidence that comes from handling a 26-foot sailboat with other new sailors.

We heartily recommend *Fast Track to Sailing* to anyone interested in taking the first steps to a new and wonderful lifestyle. Learn with a good foundation and you will enjoy sailing forever. Learn it right the first time and the rewards are incredible—and this book teaches it right. Sailing is one of the most environmentally responsible sports you can ever aspire to. Its carbon footprint is virtually invisible. Start now!

—Lex Raas
President, TUI Marine
November 2008

ACKNOWLEDGMENTS

We are forever grateful to the more than 100,000 graduates who chose the Offshore Sailing School as their path to a lifelong adventure on the water. Their praise of our programs and instructors continues to inspire all of us on the Offshore team to go the extra mile and to provide the very best sailing education there is.

The Offshore Sailing School is supported not only by the most professional faculty of instructors you'll find, but by our loyal staff behind the scenes who work diligently to make your experience flawless. The input of the entire team throughout the years has helped shape this book and match it as closely as possible to the needs and questions of new sailors.

We also thank our host partners for providing fantastic sailing venues and vacation destinations as well as beautiful cruising boats for those who dream of taking their first step to ultimate freedom—cruising under sail. We remain dedicated to our goal of making sailing the ultimate rewarding lifestyle for those who respect our world and its vast but fragile treasures.

Sailing—Good for you. Good for the World.

INTRODUCTION

The ultimate goal of many sailors is to go cruising. To help achieve that goal, we wrote the book *Fast Track to Cruising* in 2005. Because some sailors prefer to sail close to home on small to midsize sailboats, we present here an easy to read, colorful stand-alone book for the new sailor called *Fast Track to Sailing*.

You are about to embark on a most rewarding adventure, taking you from the desire to learn how to sail to ready to sail in easy, logical steps. We have always been strong proponents of learning the *right way* the first time. When I started Offshore Sailing School in 1964, I realized I was encapsulating over twenty years of intense sailing knowledge into three or four days of training. In that short time, if you absorb everything —that is, everything this book—you will gain a sailing foundation that will last a lifetime. The knowledge and methods herein give you the insight and understanding to build sailing confidence and skills. You will learn *why* you are doing something, not just how to do it. The text and illustrations provide everything you need to know to be a competent sailor. At the end of each chapter you are encouraged to test what you learned.

> *"Hands-on is a must! I discovered the best method of skill development: read the book first; practice on the boat; go home and read more; more practice."* **SUZANNE WENDEROTH (34), NORTHPORT, NY**

This book, patterned after *Fast Track to Cruising*, will teach you the basics, including the language of sailing and how it applies to maneuvers aboard, and the theory and functions that make handling a sailboat easy. You will progress from the initial steps of boarding a small to mid-size sailboat to sailing away from a dock or mooring, then to understanding how to use wind to move your boat efficiently and return safely and confidently back to a dock or mooring.

You will become skilled at controlling a boat in overpowering conditions. You will learn procedures for picking up a hat that has blown overboard or a crew member who inadvertently ended up in the water. Maneuvers such as tacking and jibing will become second nature. You will learn how to stop the boat where and when you want and how to sail backward—all without a motor, of course. You will practice the safe way to handle lines, and the proper way to ease or pull when forces and fric-

Learning to fly a spinnaker enhances your sailing.

"The Colgate 26 we used for the basic keelboat course was the right size, and at the end we were able to handle it very well. The next step was the Beneteau 464 [a 46-footer]. I had no idea what this boat would be like, but when we arrived at the marina I couldn't believe my eyes. We would maneuver this boat? It is only a matter of practice. After a few maneuvers in the harbor before leaving—that was it; the fear that I would not learn to handle this boat was gone!"
CLAUDIA LOGOTHETIS (MID-30s), DREIEICH, GERMANY

tion are involved. Learning how to navigate when there are no road signs will become as natural as driving a car on a crowded highway.

We feel that the use of a spinnaker—the colorful balloon-shaped sail—for downwind sailing enhances the sailing experience so we include it in our Learn to Sail course at Offshore Sailing School even though it is a more advanced topic. For that reason we have added the basics of spinnaker work to *Fast Track to Sailing*.

We hope you enjoy this book and keep it as a reference for future sailing. May it always be an incentive to get deeper into an activity from which you learn something new every time you sail. And when you sail, remember—you are driven by wind, not by engines requiring fuel. Sailing is the ultimate way to reduce your carbon footprint.

The authors, Doris and Steve Colgate.

GETTING TO KNOW YOUR BOAT

① *THE LANGUAGE OF SAILING*

The language of the sea is deeply rooted in the era of square-rigged ships, and today sailors around the world use a kind of shorthand that has evolved from that period. We were reminded of the importance of sailing language when we raced our 54-footer with crew from various countries. We could all communicate easily during those races—even though we didn't share a common tongue.

To the uninitiated, sailor-talk may sound strange. But it's an essential language to learn. There are times on a boat when the correct action must be taken quickly and at the right moment, or problems will result. You can't afford to say, "Let go of that thing over there!" when you really mean, "Free the jibsheet!" Through repetition, you will learn the necessary sailing terms to help you sail well.

> *"I was apprehensive about all of the language involved with sailing, but that's all gone."*
> **MARY EAMAN (37), LONGMONT, CO**

Although there are many types and sizes of sailboats, this book focuses on one type of boat—the Colgate 26, a family sport boat designed for training, racing, and family fun. The Colgate 26 is characterized as a sloop-rigged keelboat. The word *sloop* refers to a boat with one mast; the *keel* is a heavy fixed fin beneath the boat that provides stability. What you learn on this boat can be applied to any sailboat.

IMPORTANT WORDS TO KNOW

This chapter covers some key terms that are important to learn, along with summary lists that will serve as an easy reference.

If you are standing on a sailboat facing forward, you are looking at the *bow*, with the *starboard side* on your right and the *port side* on your left. Conversely, if you are facing the back end of the boat, you are facing *aft* and looking at the *stern*, with the starboard side on your left and port to your right. The widest part of a boat is called the *beam*. Some people confuse stern (the whole back end of the boat) with the word *transom*, which is the vertical or slanted part that goes from the deck to the water.

When identifying a direction, another boat, or something you need to take note of, the words *ahead*, *astern*, and *abeam* come in handy. A buoy you're looking for may be ahead, or forward of the boat. The dinghy you are towing is astern, or behind the boat. A lighthouse ashore might be abeam, at a right angle off the left or right side of the boat. "Abeam" is a word that takes on special importance when you learn to identify the proximity of other boats, especially at night, as you'll learn later.

HOW TO MEASURE A SAILBOAT

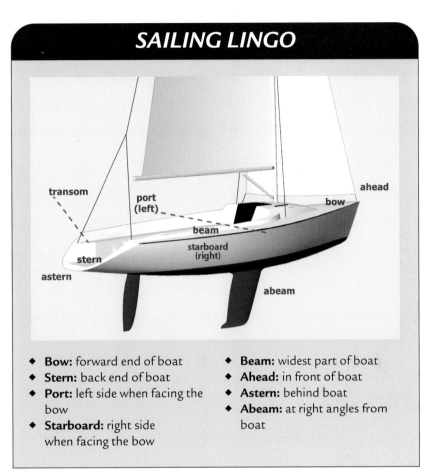

SAILING LINGO

- ◆ **Bow:** forward end of boat
- ◆ **Stern:** back end of boat
- ◆ **Port:** left side when facing the bow
- ◆ **Starboard:** right side when facing the bow
- ◆ **Beam:** widest part of boat
- ◆ **Ahead:** in front of boat
- ◆ **Astern:** behind boat
- ◆ **Abeam:** at right angles from boat

Open any sailing magazine and you will find a list of dimensions, usually abbreviated, alongside sailboat designs. These are the terms you use in describing the length, depth, and width of a sailboat.

LOA stands for *length overall*. This is the total length of the boat from the bow to the end of the stern in a straight line. LOA does not include the *bowsprit* (if your boat has one), which is a pole that extends beyond the bow of a boat. When you rent or buy a sailboat, LOA is a very common specification—as common as MPG is to a car shopper.

LWL is the *load waterline length*, or simply waterline length. This is the straight-line distance from the point where the bow emerges from the water to the point where the stern emerges from the water. Sailors need to know the LWL when calculating the potential speed of a sailboat.

Draft is the vertical distance from the water surface to the deepest part of the boat (the bottom of the keel). This measurement will tell you where you can and cannot sail. If your boat touches bottom in 3 feet of water, its draft is 3 feet. Stated differently, your boat

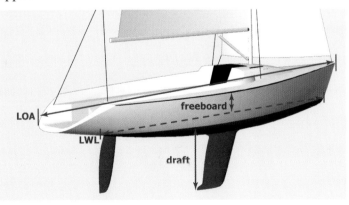

Figure 1-1. Terms that describe a boat's dimensions.

SAILING LINGO

- **LOA:** length overall (tip of bow to end of stern)
- **LWL:** load waterline length (length from bow to stern at water level when at rest)
- **Draft:** vertical depth from water surface to bottom of keel
- **Freeboard:** vertical height from water surface to edge of deck
- **Beam:** maximum width of boat
- **Hull:** body of the boat
- **Cockpit:** where the crew sits to operate the boat
- **Keel:** fin under the boat, incorporating weight for stability
- **Rudder:** underwater fin moved by the tiller to steer boat
- **Tiller:** "stick" used to steer the boat from the cockpit

draws 3 feet. When you ask a marina for a slip to rent you will probably be asked, "How much does your boat draw?" You will also be asked the LOA of your boat, because slip fees are calculated in dollars per foot.

Instead of a keel, some boats have a *centerboard*—a relatively thin panel made out of wood, fiberglass, or metal that can be raised or lowered to change the draft of the boat. In this case, you might hear someone describe the boat as having two drafts: "My boat draws 6 inches with the board up and 4 feet with the board down."

The *freeboard* of a boat, which is measured vertically from the edge of the deck to the waterline, is an important determinant of its interior space. The more freeboard a boat has, the more headroom there will be in its cabin (assuming the boat has one). Some sailors erroneously use freeboard interchangeably with the *topsides* of the boat, but the latter term actually refers to the sides of the hull above the waterline.

The beam of the boat described earlier is its maximum width, not its width at deck level as one might expect. The topsides on some boats curve outward from the deck and back in at the waterline. In this case, the beam is measured at the widest part of that curve.

HOW TO DESCRIBE A SAILBOAT

Picture yourself standing or sitting in the *cockpit*—where the crew sits to operate the boat. The *hull* is the body of the boat. The *keel*, which you can't see while you're sailing, is the fin under the boat that is loaded with lead to make the boat stable. The Colgate 26 weighs 2,600 pounds and 40 percent of that weight (1,050 pounds) is the lead in its keel. The boat can lean over in the wind, but it will not easily turn over.

In the back of the cockpit is a stick called a *tiller*. The tiller attaches to a post that goes through the hull of the boat to a *rudder*, a fin-shaped blade located underwater, behind the keel. When you move the tiller you are actually moving the rudder, which steers the boat by diverting the water that is moving past it. If the boat is not moving, turning the rudder will not cause the boat to turn.

Aboard a sailboat that has a cabin, you enter the cabin through a *companionway*—a passageway from the cockpit to the interior. The roof and sides of the cabin house comprise the *cabin trunk*.

STANDING RIGGING

Now that you are able to look at a sailboat and describe its parts, the next step is to identify rigging and what it does. *Rigging* is all the wire and rope (called line) on a sailboat and is divided into two major categories: *running rigging* and *standing rigging*. Because there is a lot of force on sails when they are filled with wind, and sails need something to hang from, rigging is required for sail support and shape.

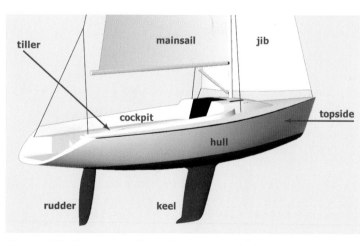

Figure 1-2. Terms that describe the parts of a sailboat.

masthead

backstay

jibstay
(here, a
forestay)

spreader

shroud

mast

boom

COLGATE 26

Figure 1-3. Terms that describe standing rigging.

RIGGING LINGO

- **Mast:** vertical spar
- **Boom:** horizontal spar, connected to the mast and supporting foot of mainsail
- **Jibstay:** wire from mast to bow; called a headstay if it goes to top of mast
- **Backstay:** wire from top of mast to deck at or near stern
- **Shrouds:** wires from mast to left and right sides of deck
- **Spreaders:** struts that increase the angle shrouds make with mast

The *mast* is the vertical pole (spar) and the *boom* is the horizontal spar. Together, they support the mainsail. Incidentally, the word *boom* is Norwegian for tree. Kevin Wensley, an Offshore Sailing School instructor who hails from England, likes to tell his students that the boom gets its name from the noise it makes when it hits you. As you will learn later, when the boom crosses the boat you always want to stay out of its way.

Standing rigging holds up the masts of a sailboat. Made out of twisted wire on small to mid-sized boats, standing rigging consists of *stays* and *shrouds*. Stays keep the mast from falling forward or backward—over the bow or the stern. Shrouds keep the mast from falling *athwartships*—over the sides of the boat.

The *backstay* runs from the *head* (top) of the mast down to the deck at the middle of the stern. The *jibstay* runs from the bow of the boat up to the top or near the top of the mast. If it leads to the head of the mast, it is a *headstay*, and the rig is called a *masthead rig*. If it leads to a point partway down the mast, it is a *forestay*, and the rig is called a *fractional rig*. Many sailors use the terms *jibstay*, *headstay*, and *forestay* interchangeably. If a wire leads from partway up the mast to the middle of the *foredeck*, between the mast and the bow, it too is called a *forestay*; but this is a complication that doesn't concern us for the time being.

Because shrouds lead from the deck edges to attachment points on the mast, the angle they make to the mast is more acute than that of the stays. For this reason, the shrouds that lead highest on the mast—the *upper shrouds*—run through the ends of a strut or tube on either side of the mast to make a wider angle. These struts or tubes are called *spreaders*, since they spread the angle the shroud makes with the mast and thus provide better support for the upper section of the mast.

The compression load on the spreaders tends to bend the mast from side to side at the spreader base. To counteract this tendency, most boats have another set of shrouds—*lower shrouds*—on either side of the mast

leading from the base of the spreaders to the edge of the deck. Since these originate lower down the mast, the angle they make with the mast is sufficiently wide to eliminate the need for extra spreaders.

RUNNING RIGGING

Running rigging consists of all the lines on a boat that adjust the sails. *Halyards* raise and lower the sails. *Sheets* adjust sails in and out.

Halyards and sheets take the name of the sail to which they are attached. For example, a *main halyard* raises and lowers the mainsail. A *jibsheet* adjusts the trim of the jib.

The trim of the jib or any sail is the angle of that sail to the wind direction at a given time. The word *trim* is also used as a verb in sailing. For example, the sailor to the left in Figure 1-4 is turning a winch (more on this later), which is moving the corner of the jib in, and he is therefore trimming the sail.

When you trim a jib, you are pulling the sail in with the jibsheet. When you *ease* a jib, you are letting it out.

When you're sailing you adjust the sheets a lot; but halyards are seldom changed after the sails are up. When you're preparing to go sailing, you raise the halyard to

Figure 1-4. Adjusting a jibsheet (running rigging) changes sail shape.

hoist the sail. Actually, you are pulling down on the halyard as the woman on deck is doing in Figure 1-5. When you are finished sailing, you ease the halyard out to lower the sail. (The halyard is actually going up.) The word *halyard* is a derivation of "haul the yardarms," from tall-ship days.

SAILS AND HOW TO DESCRIBE THEM

Today's mid-sized to large sailboats are designed with your precious time in mind, as well as your desire for an easy-to-sail boat. Regardless of size, they usually have a *mainsail* and a *jib*. On a sloop like the Colgate 26, the mainsail (pronounced *mains'l* but more often just called the *main*) is the large sail behind the mast, supported by the mast and the boom. The jib is the sail carried on the headstay or jibstay in the front of the boat.

On the Colgate 26, as on many boats these days, you control the jib with a furling mechanism that allows you to roll the sail up on its headstay when you're not using it. When a jib is on a *roller-furling headstay* like this, the jib halyard is always up. Not long ago, when you were finished sailing for the day you had to lower the halyard to bring the jib down, take the jib completely off the jibstay, fold the sail carefully to avoid wrinkles, and place it in a bag to stow below or ashore. This is still the case on most small boats and many large ones. But on some big boats, even the mainsail can be rolled up inside the mast.

Most mains and jibs are made of Dacron, which doesn't stretch much and, therefore, holds the shape of your sails. A sailmaker cuts and sews a sail to create a desirable contour for maximum speed when the sail is filled with wind. Since it is important the sail retain this shape when wind creates pressure on the cloth, sailmakers choose cloth with a predictable stretch factor, the least amount possible.

When you see a sailboat gliding along the horizon with a dazzling white sail, you're looking at Dacron. More exotic sails that are steely gray, brown-tinged, or even translucent are made of Mylar, Kevlar, or Spectra cloth. With even less stretch than Dacron, these pricey materials are in demand by highly competitive racing sailors to whom "go-fast" ability is more important than cost.

A finished sail is triangular in shape, and each corner has a name. The *head* is the top corner, the *tack* the forward lower corner, and the *clew* the aft lower corner.

Figure 1-5. Raising a sail with the halyard (running rigging).

The *luff* is the leading (front) edge, the *leech* is the trailing (aft) edge, and the *foot* is the bottom edge.

If you draw a line from the head of a mainsail to its clew, you can see that the leech is convex. When the leech of a sail is curved or rounded so as to incorporate more area than the equivalent straight-sided triangle, that extra cloth is called *roach*, and its purpose is to give you more sail area, which results in more power. To remember where the leech and roach are located on a sail,

LINGO FOR DESCRIBING SAILS

- **Mainsail:** large sail attached along mast's after edge
- **Jib:** sail carried on the head-stay or jibstay
- **Head:** top corner of a sail
- **Tack:** forward lower corner of a sail
- **Clew:** aft lower corner of a sail
- **Luff:** front edge of a sail from head to tack
- **Leech:** after edge of a sail from head to clew
- **Foot:** bottom of a sail from tack to clew
- **Battens:** slats inserted in trailing edge (leech) of sail to retain shape
- **Roach:** convex area of extra cloth along mainsail leech

Figure 1-6. Terms that describe the parts of a sail.

instructor Kevin Wensley says: *Nasty critters like roaches and leeches hang out at the back of the sail.*

To support this extra cloth and hold its shape in wind, thin pieces of wood or fiberglass called *battens* are inserted in pockets that are evenly spaced along the leech. A typical batten for a 26-foot boat might be 1 inch wide by 24 inches long. Some sails have full-length battens running all the way from leech to luff.

Sails that are furled up when not in use, rather than taken off and folded, don't have battens because they cannot be wound around a headstay or furled up inside a mast. Sails without battens do not have extra cloth (roach) along the leech. When you're out for a lazy afternoon sail or cruising off to wondrous spots, extra sail area doesn't matter that much. Ease of man-

TEST YOURSELF

Key Sailboat Terms

On the sailboat above, identify the following and then check your answers against the labeled photos and illustrations in this chapter:

1. Cockpit
2. Hull
3. Tiller
4. Bow
5. Stern
6. Port
7. Starboard
8. Beam
9. Ahead
10. Astern
11. Abeam

Describe the following:

1. LOA
2. LWL
3. Freeboard
4. Draft
5. Rudder
6. Keel

Rigging

Identify the rigging, referring to labeled photos in this chapter as necessary:

1. Mast
2. Boom
3. Jibstay
4. Backstay
5. Upper shrouds
6. Lower shrouds
7. Spreaders

The Anatomy of Sails

Identify the sails and their parts, referring to the labeled photographs in this chapter as necessary:

1. Mainsail
2. Jib
3. Battens
4. Head
5. Tack
6. Clew
7. Luff
8. Leech
9. Roach

aging the sails is more important. Roach is most helpful when performance is a priority—either for competitive sailing or for fast passages in light winds.

The only rope on a sailboat that isn't called *line* is the *boltrope*, which is sewn to the sailcloth along the foot and luff of the mainsail for reinforcement. Sometimes *sail slides* are sewn into the boltrope, and the slides literally slide the mainsail onto a track that is screwed to the mast or boom. But sail slides are usually found on larger boats; on a smaller boat, the boltrope is likely to be inserted directly inside a groove in the mast or boom when raising the mainsail.

> *"I learned so much in three days and had a great time doing it. I highly recommend the class for someone new to sailing."*
> **CHRISTINA RONAC (33), NEW YORK, NY**

To keep the leech of a sail from unraveling, the sailmaker sews a strip of doubled-over material—called *tabling*—along the edge. Sometimes a light line—the *leech cord*—is sewn inside the tabling. The leech cord is attached at the head of the sail and can be adjusted at the clew—either eased out to free a curl in the leech and permit smoother airflow, or pulled tighter to reduce the flutter that occasionally occurs along the trailing edge of a sail (especially a jib). Not only is flutter unattractive, it decreases the efficiency of a sail and eventually causes the sail cloth to wear out.

Sails are your boat's driving force. Just as an engine needs care, so do your sails. Sunlight deteriorates cloth. When not in use, sails should be taken off and put away or rolled up under a UV-protective cover. Keeping sails clean is also part of good sail care. If your sails are not washed occasionally with warm water and mild soap, encrusted salt will pick up moisture from the air and the dried salt will make your sails heavy. Dirt particles may also shorten the life of the cloth.

2 START SAILING

Weather conditions have a lot of impact on whether you will enjoy sailing. If you are dressed properly and come prepared for the best and worst conditions, you can experience the full range—from flat calm to whitecaps—in comfort.

SAILING COMFORT IS ALL ABOUT PREPARATION

Apprehensions are natural for new sailors, but you'll find that they dissolve quickly as you learn. Here are answers to some questions new sailors often ask:

What should I wear in warm sunny weather? Those who sail a lot are careful to protect skin and eyes from the sun. You might want to shed layers as the day heats up, but whatever you wear should be comfy, dry quickly, and protect you from slipping.

What should I wear if it's cold, wet, and windy? A good suit of foul-weather gear is really important, with layers underneath that breathe and shed moisture. Proper shoes, gloves, and a hat make all the difference. Think about long pants and long underwear with a shirt, sweater, and warm jacket.

What if I can't swim? There are Coast Guard–approved life vests of several types on the market that are very comfortable, and even inflatable versions you can wear like a harness or around your waist. In addition, consider learning in a sailboat that won't capsize, is easy to control in any condition, and has lifelines around the deck.

What if I'm small and not very strong? Sailing on most boats is more about timing and mechanical advantage than strength. All-women

"I really questioned whether a person 64-years-old could start learning to sail. It is a physical and mental endeavor! I can do it and so far it has been the experience of my life. I look forward to the advanced courses."
GERALD HALE (64), CAMDEN, TN

crews sail, race, and win aboard some of the largest, most challenging sailboats out there. When pulling a line, put your whole body into it, not just your arms, and place your hands over (not under) the line as you bring it toward you.

Am I too old? You can learn to sail at any age. A 92-year-old woman took Offshore Sailing School's Learn to Sail course and had a ball. She received her certificate, too.

Is sailing safe? Sailing is one of the safest pastimes there is if you know how to handle lines, winches, and sails properly. Seasoned sailors say sailing is 90 percent sheer bliss and 10 percent challenge. For the casual cruising sailor, the chances of being caught in extremely bad conditions are remote. Through this book and in hands-on sessions, you learn how to master whatever nature throws at you.

What type of boat should I learn on if my goal is to cruise? Avoid the temptation to start on a large cruising boat. You can learn much faster on a smaller, more maneuverable boat such as the Colgate 26. The process involves two steps: first, learning to sail, and then, learning to cruise. For the learn-to-sail phase, the boat should be a keelboat, unable to capsize, and unsinkable. This type of boat provides an easy transition to the more massive equipment used on a larger cruising boat. For the learn-to-cruise phase, the boat should be a popular style of boat that one might charter from one of the major charter companies or buy for personal ownership.

> "My wife is a non-swimmer and not very strong. We had a lot of fears she would not be able to handle the courses. She handled everything, including 5-foot seas, with flying colors, and she now loves to sail."
>
> **TIM GAPEN (56), WISCONSIN RAPIDS, WI**

GETTING ABOARD

The sailboat you are about to board is a dynamic platform. Whether it is tied to a dock or hanging off a mooring, it will move as you step aboard. The key is to make decisive moves, keeping your safety in mind.

If the boat is at a dock you will be walking aboard from a relatively stationary platform. If it is on a mooring, you will be boarding from a so-called taxi—a small dinghy or motor launch. The smaller the taxi, the tippier it is; when you step aboard, always step into the middle of the boat and not onto the rail or seats on the sides of the boat. The lower you place your weight in the boat, the more stable it will be. Once you're aboard, sit down immediately before someone else attempts to step in. Load the middle of the dinghy first to keep it from tipping to one side.

If any boat (the sailboat or the dinghy) has too much weight forward, which includes the crew and equipment, it is *down by the bow*. Having too much weight aft is called *dragging the stern*. Neither is good for performance, safety, or comfort. Keep the dinghy level or slightly down by the stern, and don't overload it. Remember, freeboard is the distance from the edge of the deck to the water when the boat is level. If the dinghy is so heavily loaded that its freeboard is reduced to only 6 inches or so, any rolling caused by waves or shifting passenger weight could cause the dinghy to *ship water* over its side and fill up.

Whoever is rowing the dinghy or running its outboard motor may ask you, after you are seated, to *trim the boat*. This means you should ease your weight to port or starboard to keep the dinghy level from side to side. This is called keeping a boat on an *even keel*, and it makes the boat easier to row and safer in choppy water.

Getting aboard a keelboat like a Colgate 26 is easy. Because a keelboat has a fixed fin that adds stability, you don't have to be concerned about capsizing the boat if you step on a side while boarding. If your boat has a centerboard, however, and the centerboard is in the up position, be careful to keep your weight low and in the middle of the boat as you board, just as if you were boarding a dinghy.

When you get to your sailboat, whether you board at a dock or at a mooring, the basic rules for boarding are the same:

1. If you are carrying anything, pass it across to someone onboard or throw it in the cockpit before you start to board.
2. Locate the easiest point to board—where there is a shroud you can grab and where the gap between the dock and the boat is narrowest. If the boat isn't close enough to the dock to board comfortably, find a point where you can readily pull the boat closer.
3. Make sure that whatever you grab to support yourself is fixed—not a loose line that will "give." Keep your hands and toes away from areas where they can get pinched, such as between the dock or dinghy and the sailboat.
4. The boat will probably move as you step aboard. Don't pause with one foot on the boat and the other on the dock or taxi, poised over this ever-widening split. Once you commit yourself, be decisive. The instructor in Figure 2-1 is demonstrating how *not* to board.

A good launch driver will have you board a sailboat at its middle or near its stern, where it is easier to grab something and hold the boats close together. Sometimes an eager crew member will board the sailboat near its bow and then let the boats drift apart before other crew can board. If you board first, you can help by holding the launch in close as gear is passed aboard and the rest of your party follows. If the sailboat is high-sided and there is nothing firm to grab, the safest way to board, particu-

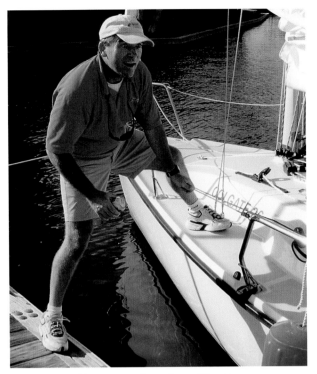

Figure 2-1. How not to board a sailboat.

larly when the water is rough, is to turn around, sit on the deck, and then swing your legs over.

GETTING READY TO SAIL

Whatever you brought aboard needs to be stowed, so find a safe place in a locker on deck or *down below* (in the cabin) where your gear won't move around or get in the way. If you haven't done so already, make sure there are enough life vests for everyone on board. Now is also a good time to reassess what you are wearing. The list below is a good reminder of the clothing adjustments you should make before you go sailing.

*   Take off any big rings and dangling bracelets or earrings.
*   Tie your hair back if it's long.
*   Put on sunscreen.
*   Secure your hat to a comfortable place on your shirt or jacket with a lanyard.
*   Put on your sailing gloves.
*   Be sure to wear a life vest or have one handy.

Life vests—or life jackets—are approved by the U.S. Coast Guard, if they are manufactured to meet or exceed specifications. Type I life jackets—the large, bulky orange horseshoes typically found on ferries and

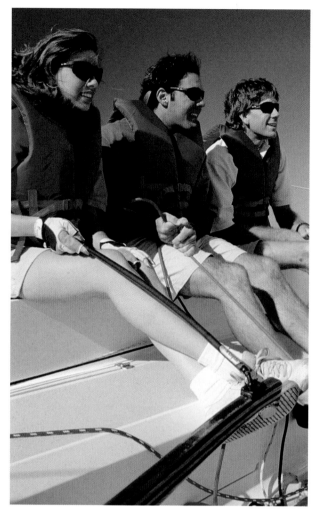

Figure 2-2. Type III life jackets.

that allows the boat to hang off or lie alongside facing the wind, that's preferable.

Check where the dock or mooring lines are tied to the boat. That way, you'll know exactly what lines you need to untie when you are ready to *cast off* (release your lines to get underway). If you have fenders hanging over the side, check to see where they are located too; all of them will have to come off as you get underway. The Colgate 26 in Figure 2-1 has a fender hanging from the boat's rail to protect the hull from contact with the dock or other boats. On some boats the rails are actually wires called *lifelines*. Locate the halyards and sheets you'll be using to pull the sails up and pull the sails in and out; make sure they are not tightly cleated or jammed in a block. Assign jobs to your crew, and position yourself comfortably to execute your jobs.

Preparing the Sails

Since so many sailboats allow you to leave the sails rigged (but not raised) on the boat, this section starts from that premise.

You will typically have a sail cover over the mainsail, which has been folded (or *furled*) on the boom at the sail's foot. The cover will be tied or hooked at intervals beneath the boom. Remove the sail cover by folding it repeatedly, starting at the after end of the boom; then stow it below or in a cockpit locker. You should now see the mainsail neatly folded and tied onto the boom.

You will see a stiffener, or *headboard*, in the head of the mainsail. Attach the main halyard to the grommet hole in the headboard and pull up on the halyard just enough to get a little tension. You should still have three or four sail ties holding the mainsail in place along the boom. Untie these now and stow them.

Before you hoist the sail, look up to make sure the halyard is running free and not wrapped around anything. Make sure your boat is headed directly into the wind. If you try to raise a sail when the wind is at an angle to the boat or coming from behind, you will have a devilish time trying to haul against the pressure of the wind in the sail. And while you're preoccupied with this challenge, your boat will be trying to sail around its mooring.

You're raising the mainsail first because it's nearer the stern and can act like a weather vane to keep the boat headed into the wind. If your boat was attached to a mooring or at anchor and you raised the jib first, the jib would fill with wind and force the bow to turn away. Eventually the boat would swing broadside to the wind

cruise ships—are made to keep an unconscious person face up in the water. A Type II life jacket, called a near-shore buoyant vest, is less bulky, less buoyant, and not as likely to keep an unconscious person face up. Type III, the type of vest the sailors are wearing in Figure 2-2, is probably the most popular life jacket because it is fairly comfortable to wear; but it will not do much for an unconscious person. Type IV is a throwable flotation device such as a cushion. Type V is inflatable.

Preparing the Boat

Take a few minutes to look around. Try to determine where the wind is coming from, and position the boat with its bow in that direction if you can. If you're at a mooring, the boat should already be pointing into the wind, since that's its natural tendency when tethered from the bow. If you're at a dock and can move to a spot and strain at the mooring line, creating a general nuisance. If you were to forge ahead by raising the mainsail, it too would fill with wind and press against the rigging and bind on the mast track. This would make it virtually impossible to raise the sail any farther.

When raising a sail, you want the lines that control the sail to be loose so the boat (and sail) can line up with the wind like a flag. All lines that might be holding the boom down—principally the mainsheet, but also the boom vang and cunningham (if you have these on your boat)—must be eased so nothing can prevent the main from going all the way up (we'll discuss the boom vang and cunningham in good time). A crew member should hold the back end of the boom up in the air to relieve the tension on the leech of the sail.

You will know the sail is all the way up when the luff (the edge attached to the mast track) is taut, with no scallops or horizontal wrinkles. When the main is up, *cleat* (tie off) the halyard so the sail can't slip back down, but leave the mainsheet loose while you get the jib ready. Watch out for the boom swinging back and forth, particularly on a windy day.

Next, *unfurl* (unroll) the jib. Note that the jib halyard is already attached and that the two jibsheets, which lead back to the cockpit on either side of the mast, are wrapped around the rolled sail. The drum at the bottom of the sail has a line leading all the way back to the cockpit, where it is normally cleated; the excess is typically coiled up and hung on a lifeline to keep it out of the way when the jib is not in use. To unfurl the jib, all you have to do is uncleat this furling line and pull on the jibsheet.

If you do not have a roller-furling jib, you must *hank* (attach) the sail on the jibstay with piston hanks or snaps spaced along the luff of the sail. The jib should have been folded starting with the foot, then rolled so the tack is on the outside. After removing the jib from its bag, find the tack and attach it to the fitting in the bow at the bottom of the headstay. Then, straddling the sail with your legs to keep it under control, place each hank on the stay working up the luff to the head of the sail. Then tie port and starboard jibsheets to the clew of the sail with bowlines and *reeve* (pull) them through the jibsheet leads. Attach the halyard and hoist.

Some boats have a *jib foil*—a slotted tube into which the luff slides. In this case, start with the head of the sail, attach the halyard and feed the luff of the jib into the groove of the foil while one crew raises the halyard. Often you'll find a prefeeder, a small device that

Figure 2-3. Attaching halyard to the head of the sail.

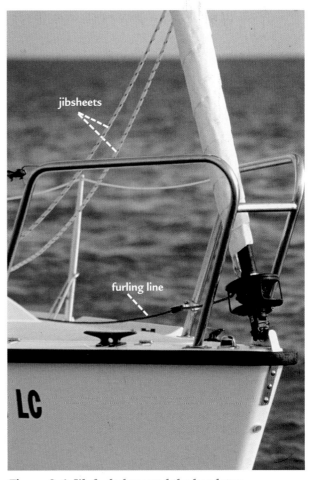

jibsheets

furling line

LC

Figure 2-4. Jib furled around the headstay.

KNOTS TO KNOW

The ends of most sheets have knots in them to keep the sheet from running completely out of the *blocks* (the pulleys that sheets run through) and out of your reach. The two most common *stopper knots* used in the ends of jibsheets and mainsheets are the *figure eight* and the *stop knot*.

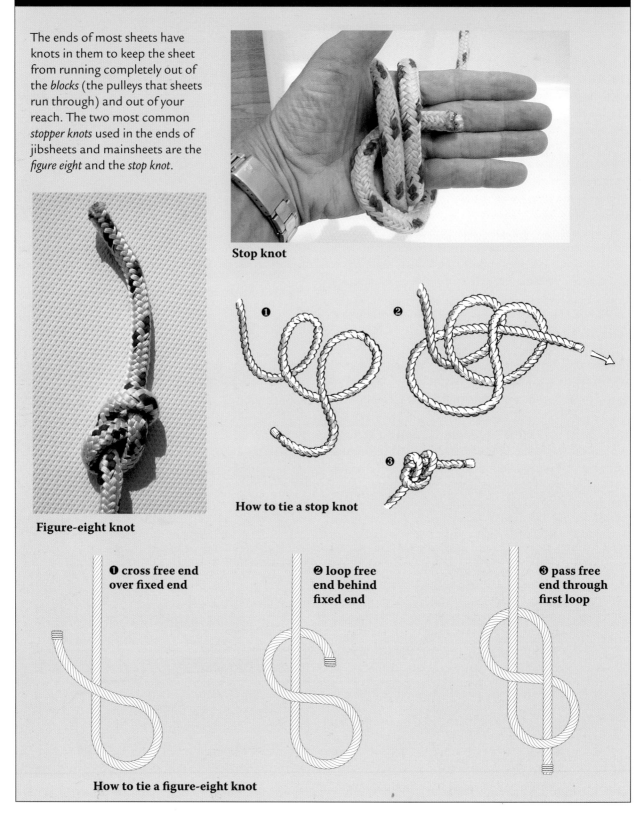

Stop knot

Figure-eight knot

How to tie a stop knot

❶ **cross free end over fixed end**

❷ **loop free end behind fixed end**

❸ **pass free end through first loop**

How to tie a figure-eight knot

automatically feeds the luff into the groove. This is the same process you'll go through when initially raising the jib on a roller-furling jib foil.

Since one jibsheet leads aft along the port side of the boat and the other to starboard, which sheet do you pull on? It really doesn't matter until you get underway, but if you know which side of the boat the wind will be coming over, pull on the jibsheet farthest from the wind (the *lee-ward* jibsheet), unless you need to *back* the jib as described later in this chapter.

On small boats, where the jib is smaller than the mainsail, you could raise the two sails simultaneously; but it's good protocol to raise the jib last so it won't flail around. Not only does this flogging tangle the jibsheets and cause an awful commotion on a windy day, it also reduces the life of the jib by breaking down the cloth fibers.

GETTING UNDERWAY

Now you're ready to sail away. But since the boat is headed directly into the wind at a mooring and is not moving through the water, how are you going to do this? The boat is dead in the water, or *in irons*. When the bow is headed into the wind like this, you are in the *no-go zone*.

This can happen at other times too. For example, when a boat attempts to change direction by turning into the wind, it can be stopped by a wave and lose *steerage* or *headway*. In order to steer a boat, you need to have water flowing past its rudder. If the boat is *dead in the water,* meaning it's motionless, the rudder is useless. The sails have to be manipulated to get the boat going.

Because the boat is pointing directly into the wind, the sails are *luffing*—flapping in the wind like a flag. To fill the sails, you will have to place the boat at an angle of 45° or more to the wind. When the boat reaches this position the sails will fill with wind and the boat will start moving forward. Until that point, the sails have to be manually forced out against the wind to fill them. This is called *backing* the sail.

If you want to turn the bow of the boat to port (to the left), back the jib out to starboard; if pulling on the starboard-side jibsheet won't accomplish this, you'll have to grab the clew of the jib and literally hold it out to starboard until it backs. Once the wind hits the starboard side of the jib, it will push the bow to port. After the boat is pushed 45° to the wind, release the starboard-side jibsheet and pull in on the sheet on the port side.

Though backing the jib is the fastest and surest method of falling off onto the desired tack, there are other ways. If the boat is drifting backward and you want to change direction and sail forward and to the right, push the tiller to the starboard side of the boat. The rudder turns the stern of the boat to the left and the bow moves to the right.

Figure 2-5. Backing the jib to get underway.

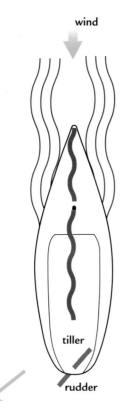

Figure 2-6. How to get going when the boat is drifting backward. Here, the bow will fall off to starboard.

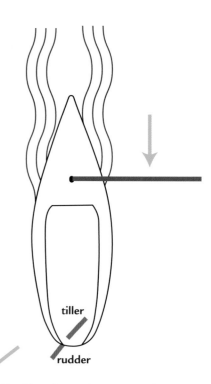

Figure 2-7. Backing the main to get underway.

FROM NO-GO TO GO

When a sailboat is motionless:

- It is *in irons* or *in stays*
- Water is not flowing past the rudder
- And the rudder therefore can't steer boat

To get out of irons:

- Back the jib to one side
- The bow will swing to the opposite side
- When the bow is 45 or more degrees off the wind, trim the sails for the wind direction
- Steer with the rudder

You might be sailing a small boat that has no jib. In that case you can push the main out against the wind. This starts the boat moving backward and turns the stern to the side opposite the main. If you *back* the main to the starboard side, the stern will go to port. You can abet the turn by putting the tiller to starboard.

The standard procedure when leaving a mooring is for one of the crew to untie the mooring line, but hold onto the end while another crew backs the jib. If possible, pull the boat forward with the mooring line to gain a little forward momentum. Sometimes it helps to *scull* the boat to start the boat moving forward. To scull, move the tiller rapidly back and forth. This causes the rudder to move like a flipper, resulting in forward motion. (On the Colgate 26 you can actually turn the rudder 180° and scull the boat backward out of a slip or away from a dock.) When the bow is definitely swinging in the desired direction, release the mooring line and you are off sailing.

STEERING

Taking command of a sailboat is one of the most delightful things you'll ever do. There's simply nothing like feeling your boat's pulse as it cuts through the water and the way it responds to your slightest moves on the helm.

Most new sailors learn on boats steered with a tiller, often referred to as the *stick* by seasoned sailors. The tiller, positioned in the back of the cockpit

Figure 2-8. Steering with a tiller.

where you'll sit if you're steering, is attached to a rudder under the boat. It's the deflection of water against the rudder that determines the boat's direction as it moves. As the rudder's angle to the flow of water changes, so does the sailboat's direction. The extent to which you push or pull the tiller determines how much deflection there will be, which translates into how fast or far you'll turn the boat.

At first, steering with a tiller might seem unnatural; but it's the best way to learn because you can really *sense* how the boat reacts to you. Most boats up to 30 feet in length have tillers, not wheels, so it's appropriate that you start out on a boat with a tiller like the Colgate 26. When you step aboard a cruising boat later on, you will get behind a wheel and drive that boat as you would a car—but you'll have the fingertip control of somebody who learned to steer a sailboat first with a tiller.

A sailboat responds best when you can feel a slight tug as you hold the tiller. The only time you want a *neutral helm*—no pressure at all—is when you are sailing in a straight line with the wind directly behind the boat.

> *"Relax. That's the one thing impressed on us. Don't stress, or you tighten your hold too much on the sheets [and] overturn the tiller."*
>
> **SHARON MARION (49), SAN JOSE, CA**

TILLER STEERING TIPS

- *Tiller Toward Trouble*—push the tiller *toward* trouble, and the bow turns *away*
- Push the tiller to the right (to starboard) to turn the boat left (to port)
- Push the tiller left (to port) to turn the boat right (to starboard)
- Avoid oversteering—make minimal, smooth moves
- If you are fighting the tiller, consider easing the sails

Figure 2-9. The rudder is visible in the clear waters of BVI; the crew sits to windward for comfort and balance.

When sails are trimmed correctly, you can hold the tiller with a light touch. The rudder is in line with or at a very slight angle to the keel. The resistance you feel is normal and desired. If you find yourself fighting the tiller, your rudder is probably at too great an angle and actually slowing the boat and diminishing its performance.

If you have ever driven a car that needs its wheels aligned, you will remember how hard it was to keep the car in a straight line without a strong pull on the wheel. This causes you to oversteer, and that's what you are doing when you have too much tug on the tiller. Adjusting the sails usually cures this. In Chapter 5 you will learn more about helm balance.

A sailboat pivots as it turns, with the stern going one way and the bow the other. If you are sitting to the left of the tiller, holding it with your right hand, and you want the boat to turn to the right—to *starboard*—pull the tiller toward you, to the left. Water pushes against the right side of the rudder, which moves the stern to the left and pivots the bow to the right. If you want the boat to turn to the left—to *port*—push the tiller away from you, to the right. Water pushes against the left side of the rudder, which moves the stern to the right and pivots the bow to the left. At first you might have to think about which way to push the tiller, but eventually, steering with a tiller will become automatic.

Note in Figure 2-9 that the sails are over the port side of the boat and everyone is sitting on the starboard side. Not only are they having fun, they are using crew weight to balance the boat. Picture yourself steering and turn the tiller to starboard, in this case toward you. The rudder turns to port, and so does the boat. Now push the tiller away from you, to port. The rudder turns to starboard, and so does the boat.

The keel is heavy, carrying a lot of weight down low. As wind fills the sail and tries to heel the boat over, the keel counteracts this force and keeps the boat moving forward without tipping over or sliding sideways. As you sail along, always watch for other boats and obstacles that might cause trouble.

MAKE YOURSELF COMFORTABLE

When you're learning to sail, you'll probably sail with two to three other crew and rotate positions as you go through maneuvers. Since comfort is key to handling yourself and the boat well, here are a few tips:

1. When steering, sit on the high (windward) side of the boat if it's heeling (tilting or leaning to one side or the other), so you can see the luff of the jib.
2. Ask the crew to join you on the high side when they are finished with their jobs—for their own comfort and to help counteract the heeling effect and better balance the boat.
3. Assign someone to go down to the lower side periodically to look to leeward and make sure you're clear of other boats and obstructions.
4. Always sit so that you can move the tiller freely from side to side without it hitting your body. Usually this means sitting slightly forward of the end of the tiller.
5. To maximize the arc through which the tiller can move, and to give yourself maximum leverage, hold the tiller at or close to its free end.
6. Avoid white-knuckle syndrome—relax and hold the tiller tenderly. A tight fist around the tiller tightens your forearm and puts stress on your upper body, and you end up steering from your shoulder with jerky results, and not comfortably with your wrist.
7. When moving from one side of the boat to the other while steering, always pass in front of the tiller and look forward for better control. This allows you to see your crew and other boats in the vicinity.
8. Before changing course, give your crewmates plenty of warning so that they can position themselves to trim the sails comfortably.
9. When *tacking* (see Chapter 3), work at the same pace as the crew and slow your turn as the sail comes across, giving the crew time to complete their jobs and then move to a comfortable position.
10. When *jibing* (Chapter 3), give your crewmates plenty of time to get the mainsail under control before you turn, and make sure everyone is aware of the pending maneuver and out of the way of the swinging boom.
11. If the winds are very light, you and your crew should sit on the low side (leeward) to induce a heel to leeward, thus encouraging the sails to hold their shape and capture what little wind there is (see more on this in Chapter 5). If you can't see the jib from this position, however, sit elsewhere and let your crew heel the boat.

TEST YOURSELF

Steering Basics
To test what you now know about steering, answer the questions below. Refer back to the steering section in this chapter if you need to review these concepts.

1. What does the rudder do?
2. What does the tiller do?
3. Where is the no-go zone?
4. If you are dead in the water, how do you start moving the boat forward?
5. If you move the tiller to port, where does the bow go?
6. If you move the tiller to starboard, what direction does the rudder go?

3 THE POINTS OF SAIL

"Fabulous adventure! I learned so much and am looking forward to using my new skills."
TARA SCARLETT (35), ATLANTA, GA

Sailing is a lot like riding a bicycle. When you finally catch on, you never lose the knack. Just as balance is the most important skill in bicycling, feeling the relationship between the wind and the sails is the key to sailing.

The *points of sail* describe the boat when it is sailing at various angles to the wind direction. Diagrams that illustrate the points of sail (like the ones that follow) show the wind as nice clear arrows. This may be easy to illustrate on paper; but on the water, it may be hard to relate the boat's heading to the wind direction.

FINDING WIND DIRECTION

Sails are a sailboat's engine, and the wind is that engine's fuel. Until you know where the wind is coming from, you won't be able to fully utilize the wind's power. However, once you become sensitive to wind direction, you never lose that capability.

Since you can't see the wind, you have to use other tricks to detect its direction. Look at ripples on the water. Feel the wind on your face: when you look directly into the wind, you can feel it evenly on both sides of your face; turn even slightly and you know right away you are no longer looking at the source of the wind. You can also look for smoke or flags on land. Sailors use many other aids to find wind direction, including electronic instrumentation. The simplest aids are *telltales* and a *masthead fly*.

Telltales are pieces of wool, thin strips of plastic, or other light materials tied to the shrouds; they show the wind direction by the way they flow away from the shroud. A masthead fly is a swiveling weather vane at the top of the mast with an arrow on one end and a split tail on the other. To find the wind, look up and follow the direction the arrow is pointing. The masthead fly is very light to avoid extra weight at the top of the mast; extra weight aloft will contribute to how far your boat *heels*, or leans over. The masthead fly's light weight is also important because it makes this aid more sensitive to the wind in very light breezes. In most conditions, it will turn easily to a new wind direction and settle down quickly—rather than swinging past the new direction, due to inertia.

YOUR BOAT IS ALWAYS ON A TACK

To describe the direction of the wind with respect to the sails, sailors use the word *tack*. A boat is always *on a tack* unless it is in the process of changing tacks (changing the boat's direction from one side of the wind to the other, while sailing toward the wind). The word tack also has other meanings: as you learned earlier, the word *tack* is also used to describe the forward, lower corner of a sail.

One way to remember which tack you are on is to identify the wind's direction as it comes across the boat. If the wind comes over the port side of the boat, you are on a *port tack*. If it comes over the starboard side, you are on a *starboard tack*.

This method of determining what tack you are on works well unless the wind is directly behind your boat. In this case you are sailing *downwind* and the wind is coming over the back, or stern, of your boat. When sailing downwind, you need to look at where your main boom is located to determine what tack you are on.

Your main boom is either over the port or starboard side of the boat. The rule to remember is: a boat is on the tack *opposite* to the side its main boom is on. For example, if your mainsail is over the starboard side of the boat, you are on port tack. If your mainsail is over the port side of the boat, you are on starboard tack. If your boom is pulled in tight and very close to the

Figure 3-1. A sailboat on port tack.

Figure 3-2. A sailboat on starboard tack.

boom on starboard

wind

Figure 3-3. A sailboat on port tack on a run.

TACK: A WORD WITH SEVERAL MEANINGS

1. Tack *n* **1** : forward lower corner of a sail **2** : boat's heading in relation to the wind <on a starboard ~> **3** : a course <when the boat is underway it's on a ~>
2. Tack *vb* : to change direction from one side of wind to the other while sailing toward the wind

center of the boat, making it difficult for you to determine which side the boom is on, simply picture which side the boom will be on if you ease the sail out.

Figure 3-3 helps to better illustrate how to determine the tack you are on when sailing downwind. In the photo, the wind is blowing toward the boat's stern and the boat is on a *run*—sailing away from the wind. Note that the boom is over the starboard side of the boat. Remember, the tack the boat is on is the *opposite* side of the boat the boom is on. This boat is on *port tack*.

Another way to determine which tack you are on is to look at how the wind is filling the mainsail. If the wind is filling the port side of the main-sail, you are on port tack. If it is filling the starboard side of the mainsail, you are on starboard tack.

Just like cars on the road, sailboats on the water also have their own right-of-way rules. Knowing what tack you are on is important because it determines which boat has the right-of-way. (You'll learn what these rules are and when to observe them in Chapter 8.)

CYCLING THROUGH THE POINTS OF SAIL

To get to your destination, you have to ease and trim your sails in relation to the direction of the wind. The relationship between your boat's *heading* (the direction it's going) and the wind direction represents a point of sail and determines how you set your sails. To easily see the relationship between a boat's heading and the wind direction, each point of sail is marked on the circle in Figure 3-4.

These points of sail start with the no-go zone where the boat cannot sail directly into the wind and must *tack* (change from port to starboard tack, or vice versa). When the sails are trimmed in as tight as possible, the boat is *close-hauled.* Sometimes they will be as far out as they can go as you sail downwind on this point of sail, the wind is pushing you from behind. As the boat sails from a close-hauled course, the closest it can possibly sail toward the wind, to a downwind run, the farthest it can sail off the wind, the boat is *falling off*—sailing away from the wind.

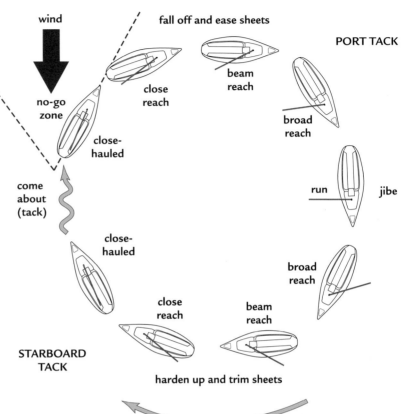

Figure 3-4. Points of sail.

As you see on the diagram, as the boat falls off from a close-hauled course and heads downwind, it cycles through a point of sail called a *reach.* There are several different types of reaches. Here is an exercise to help you understand the relationship between the wind direction and your heading on a reach.

Point the bow of the boat close to the direction of the wind, but not quite to the no-go zone. Then point your arm at the wind direction and start falling off, turning your bow away from the wind direction. Keep your arm pointed at the wind direction.

When the angle between your arm and your heading is about 60°, you are on a *close reach*—a point between sailing as close to the wind as possible and when the wind is at a right angle, or 90°, to your boat.

Keep falling off until your arm is at a 90° angle to your heading. You are now sailing with the wind *abeam* on a *beam reach.*

The easiest point of sail to practice on is a reach. This is a good point of sail for getting comfortable with steering. The boat won't heel excessively and you can wander off course without the boom accidentally flying across the boat, or *jibing* (which we will cover soon).

Figure 3-5. A close reach.

Figure 3-6. A beam reach.

TO TRIM FOR EFFICIENT SAILING

- *Ease* sheet until sail starts to *luff*
- *Trim* the sheet until luffing stops
- When in doubt, let it out

On a beam reach your telltales should be streaming right across the boat. Now point your arm at the wind and turn the boat slightly toward the direction you are pointing. This takes you back onto a close reach. As you continue to turn toward the wind, your sails start to luff (flutter) and you need to pull them in to keep them full of wind. When you adjust your sails for wind direction and strength, you are *trimming* your sails.

Picture the sail like a flag waving in the breeze. If you grab the tail of the flag and pull it toward the wind it will fill with air and stop flapping. In essence, you are trimming it by pulling it in. As you let the flag go slowly (like easing a sail) it will start to flutter where it first lines up with the wind. So, as you sail along on a reach, make little adjustments to determine whether your sails are trimmed properly. Ease the sail until it starts to luff at the leading edge (naturally called the *luff* of the sail), and then trim it back until the luffing stops.

Instructor Michelle Boggs uses another tip for trimming sails: *When in doubt, let it out.* This is a good one to remember when reaching. The sail may look perfectly fine, but it may actually be trimmed too tight, which makes the boat heel more and sail slower than it should.

Figure 3-7. A broad reach.

Figure 3-8. Close-hauled.

Now that you have the feel of sailing on a close reach and a beam reach, the next step is to experience a *broad reach*—the point between a *beam reach* and sailing dead downwind. The wind is on your quarter (aft of abeam) and you have to concentrate a little more on your steering because, at this point, it is easy to go off course without realizing it. If you turn the boat so the wind ends up directly behind you, the mainsail looks perfectly fine but you are no longer on a broad reach. You are now on a run.

COMMANDS FOR CHANGING COURSE WITHOUT JIBING OR TACKING

- *Harden up* or *come up*—turn the boat toward the wind
- *Head down* or *fall off*—turn the boat away from wind

Turn the boat back toward the direction of the wind—from a broad reach to a beam reach. If you point your arm at the wind again and continue turning the boat in that direction, you will have to continue trimming the sails to keep them from luffing. When you can't trim the sails any tighter because they are almost in the middle of the boat, you are back to sailing close-hauled—which again is sailing as close to the wind as possible without actually luffing. Most sailboats sail an average of 45° to the wind on a close-hauled course.

When you are on a reach, the crew is responsible for keeping the sails full by adjusting them in or out while you steer a straight course. When you are close-hauled, it is up to the person steering to keep the sails full. If you are steering a close-hauled course and the sails start to flutter or go soft along the leading edge, you are probably *sailing too high*, too close to the direction of the wind. This is also called *pinching*. To fill the sails properly, head away (fall off) from the wind just enough to stop the luffing. Continually test your course by heading up slightly until the jib (or mainsail if you only have one sail) starts to luff, and then head off just a bit until the sail looks firm.

Sailors use many terms to describe a boat's course in relation to the wind, but those that have the connotation of *up* or *high* imply you are sailing too close to the wind. *Down* or *low* imply being away or too far from the wind—more broadside to it. If someone says, "You're too high," you are too close to the wind and your sails are either luffing slightly or will soon start to luff.

We have already learned the term *falling off*. Again, when you fall off from a close-hauled position to a reach, you are sailing away from the wind. Your crew might also say to you, "Head down," to indicate you are sailing too high and need to fall off. The opposite is to *harden up*. When you harden up from a reach to a close-hauled course, you are sailing more toward the wind.

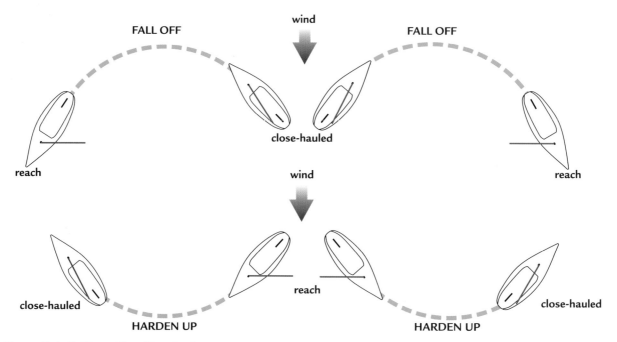

Figure 3-9. Falling off and hardening up.

If you are sailing too far away from the wind and your crew wants you to harden up, they might also tell you to "come up."

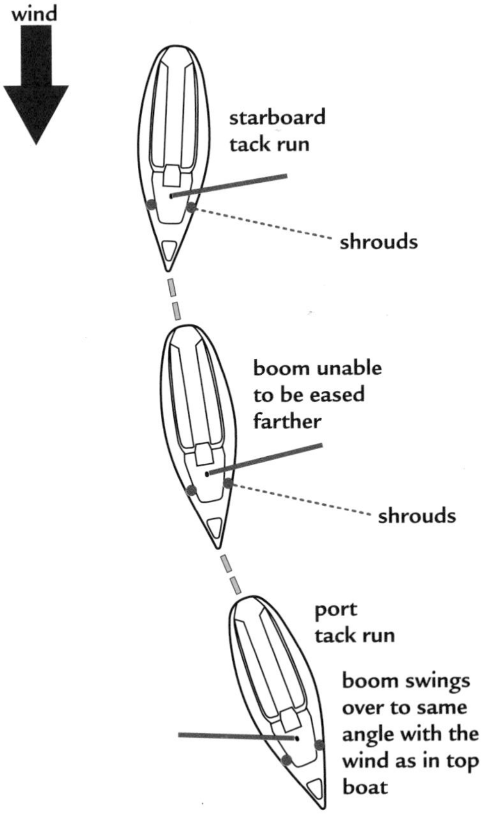

CHANGING COURSE DOWNWIND

A *run* or *running free* is essentially sailing with the wind pushing the boat from behind. When you fall off from close-hauled to reaching, you ease the sails to maintain a consistent angle to the wind. As you fall off to a run, however, you reach a point when you can't ease the sail out any farther because the boom is against the shrouds that hold up the mast. If you want to turn farther, you will have to *jibe* and bring the boom over to the other side of the boat.

When the boom crosses the centerline of the boat—an imaginary line from the bow to the middle of the stern—you have changed tacks. Any change of tack from port to starboard or vice versa while sailing downwind is called a *jibe*. When sailing downwind, the bow turns away from the source of the wind and the wind comes over the stern. Just changing course downwind is not jibing. Until the boom crosses the centerline, you are simply falling off—turning away from the wind while staying on the same tack.

You will give your crew specific commands during a jibe. On the command, "Prepare to jibe," the crew's job is to start pulling in the mainsheet. It is safer and easier to bring the boom toward the center of the boat as the person steering starts the jibe; this way, the boom has a shorter distance to travel when it swings across. When the wind starts to fill the back side of the mainsail, the boom will come across with fury—and woe to anyone who gets in its path. By trimming it in first, the crew keeps the swing of the boom to a minimum. When you see the boom near the middle of the boat, give the command, "Jibe ho!" and turn the boat. As soon as the boom crosses the boat's centerline, the crew should let out the mainsheet quickly on the other side to keep the boat from heeling excessively.

Don't be alarmed if you start to turn the boat the wrong way in a jibe. New sailors often do this, but it can be corrected easily. The proper direction jibes the boat. The wrong direction causes the boat to *round up* on the same tack toward the wind. Just remember to turn the bow toward the end of the boom when jibing and you will be fine.

Because of the distance the boom has to travel across the boat when jibing, a major concern is that the boom might swing across unexpectedly. This is called an *accidental jibe*, and it can happen when the skipper unintentionally veers off course or a wind shift occurs. The wind ends up on the same side of the boat as the main boom and pushes the boom across.

The process of jibing varies with different sailboats. Some sailors throw the boom over to the other side rather than trim it in. But until you know the capabilities of your boat, the safest way to jibe is the prudent way—as described above.

A run is a "warm" point of sail, as

Figure 3-10. Jibing is changing tacks downwind.

wind

starboard
tack run

shrouds

boom unable
to be eased
farther

shrouds

port
tack run

boom swings
over to same
angle with the
wind as in top
boat

COMMANDS FOR JIBING

To prepare the crew, say "Prepare to jibe!" When the crew answers "okay," say "Jibe ho!"

INSTRUCTOR TIP

"To avoid an accidental jibe: Tiller to the boom to avoid doom."
MANAGER OF OFFSHORE SAILING SCHOOL, CAPTIVA ISLAND, FL

Figure 3-11. Sailing on a run.

the wind is from behind, going with you. In Figure 3-11, all the boats are on a run, sailing downwind. The wind is coming from behind; the sails are all the way out. What tack are they on?

When the wind gets on the wrong side of the sails on a boat like a Colgate 26, which has a main and jib, the jib starts to dance and an accidental jibe can occur. In Figure 3-12, Boat A is sailing with the wind on the opposite side of the boat from the boom, the jib is full, and there is no fear of an accidental jibe. Boat B is sailing dead (directly) downwind, and the jib is looking soft because the main is blocking the wind; but this boat is in no danger of jibing unless you steer sloppily or a wave throws the stern to one side.

Boat C is sailing *by the lee,* with the wind on the same side of the boat as the boom. Though dangerous, a boat can sail along like this with the wind coming over the *leeward* side of the boat. You might think this would make it the windward side because the wind is now hitting that side first; to avoid confusion, right-of-way rules define the *leeward side* as the side over which the main boom is carried.

Boat D has sailed too far by the lee. The wind will catch the other side of the mainsail and throw it across the boat in what is often called a *flying,* or accidental, jibe. The boom rises up in the air unless held down by a *boom vang,* and the wind fills the other side of the sail and causes an accidental jibe. Note that the jib is already crossing to the other side of the boat: this is your first

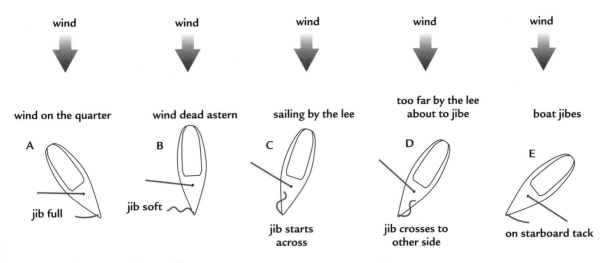

Figure 3-12. How an accidental jibe occurs.

warning of an accidental jibe. When the jib crosses to the other side, the main isn't far behind—so watch out! To avoid this, head slightly higher. Boat E has jibed and is now on starboard tack. After jibing, you can steer any course on starboard tack all the way up to close-hauled just by hardening up. Try this often. It's a great exercise in learning the feel of different points of sail.

We knew a grand lady everyone called Aunt Nan, who, well before it was accepted, almost always sailed with an all-women crew. She often invited complete novices to crew. When she was in her 70s, one of her beginner crew was assigned the job of trimming in the mainsail for the jibe around a racing mark. The rest of the crew, who were more experienced, took care of the difficult tasks. Before the race, Aunt Nan carefully described the new sailor's job: "Trim the mainsail with the mainsheet, but don't make it fast," which meant don't cleat the mainsheet or secure it to something. Just before the mark she gave the command, "Prepare to jibe!" The new crew member started pulling in the mainsheet hand over hand at a snail's pace. Terribly agitated because they were barreling down on the mark with boats at close quarters all around them, Aunt Nan cried, "Hurry up!" She then received an extremely haughty reply: "But you said, don't make it fast!"

Sailing terms may seem confusing at first, but proper communication on a boat not only makes sailing more fun, it is an absolute necessity when swift action is required.

SAILING TOWARD THE WIND

You want to reach a destination that is directly upwind of your boat. But when your destination is a point that makes you sail toward the wind, you won't go anywhere but backward if you sail directly into the wind (remember the no-go zone). Therefore, you have to *tack* back and forth to get to your destination.

You know by now that you can't sail closer to the wind than 45°. So to get to that upwind point, you sail a zig-zag course—first on one tack and then on the other, until you reach your destination. Each turn you make from port to starboard and then starboard to port is a *tack*. As you maneuver

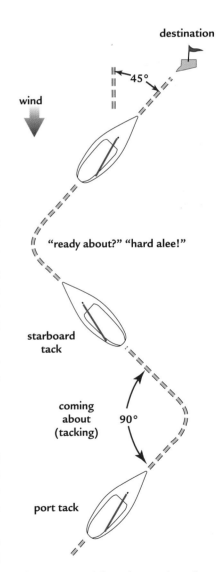

Figure 3-13. A beat is a series of tacks.

UNDERSTANDING WINDWARD AND LEEWARD

leeward side   windward side

wind

The *windward* side of anything is the side from which the wind arrives. The *leeward* side (pronounced *looward*) is the side from which the wind departs. If a wind-propelled beachball hit your boat on the starboard side, that side would be the windward side and the other side the leeward side. If the beachball went on to hit another boat after yours, your boat is the windward boat and the next boat is the leeward boat. The same holds true for windward or leeward islands, marks, or other objects on the water.

upwind each change from one tack to the other is called *coming about*. A series of tacks is called a *beat* or *beating to windward*.

Once again, you will give specific commands to prepare the crew for a successful change of course. Alert the crew first by saying, "Stand by to come about," or "Ready about!" The crew's main job now is to get the jib ready for the tack by uncleating it—but not yet releasing it—and preparing to pull on the opposite jibsheet. As long as you are in open water with no other boats or obstructions around, the mainsail, which is near the middle of the boat when close-hauled, can be left to travel the short distance on its own. There is usually no need to adjust it. However, a crew member should always be prepared to release the mainsheet.

When your crew responds "Ready!", start turning while giving the command "Hard alee!" Now you push the tiller to leeward (away from the wind) for the tack, and the bow turns toward the wind. When you point to the wind and turn the bow in that direction, you are tacking. Remember the two "Ts"—Tack Toward the wind. The command for tacking—"hard alee!"—is an Americanization of the old "helm's alee!" which meant the helm (the tiller) was put to the leeward side of the boat.

When you are sailing close-hauled, figure out where you want to end up before you tack. If you are on port tack and want to change to starboard tack, look directly out (abeam) to port. Find a landmark in that vicinity and plan to end up with your bow pointing at that landmark when you complete the tack.

WHEN TACKS DON'T GO AS PLANNED

The good news is that you now understand the theory of tacking upwind; the bad news is that tacks don't always go according to plan. That is, until

COMMANDS FOR TACKING

To prepare crew ask, "Ready about?" When they answer yes, say "Hard alee!"

Figure 3-14. The lead boat is head to wind, and its sails are luffing; the boat behind has trimmed sails.

REDUCE HEELING AND HEELING FEARS

If someone on your boat is afraid of heeling, which is not uncommon at first, let that person handle the mainsheet so they can control the amount of heel themselves. In a short time, a fearful crew will understand they are truly in control and start to enjoy sailing in strong winds with great confidence.

Another way to reduce heeling is to reduce the wind's force on your sails by heading into the wind and allowing the sails to luff slightly. In small doses this is called *feathering* the boat to windward; but in response to a strong gust it is simply luffing.

you understand the mechanics of changing tacks. (If other boats are close by, always be prepared to release the mainsheet quickly. If you do not release or ease the mainsheet when you fall off to avoid a collision, your boat will heel excessively, rendering the rudder ineffective because so much of it will be out of the water. In short, falling off will be difficult.)

For example, you might fail to complete a tack and your boat ends up dead in the water, or *head to wind*. The bow is pointed into the wind and the boat is motionless. Without motion there is no water flowing past the rudder. Remember that when you were leaving a mooring, the rudder had to deflect water in order to turn the boat. If you aren't moving, your boat has no *steerageway*. Turning the rudder doesn't turn the boat. You are *in irons*.

You know if your boat is about to stop when the sails start to luff and stream aft like a flag. Usually this happens when you allow the boat to slow up too much before attempting to tack. A wave can stop the boat in the middle of the tack leaving you with no *way on*, a temporary condition. The boat will shortly fall off to one tack or the other, but you may not end up on the desired tack.

If, for instance, the reason for the tack was a moored boat dead ahead, it could be very embarrassing (and costly) to get in irons and then fall back on the same tack. Since your boat can't gain any steerageway until it gains speed, by the time you are moving enough to try to tack again, you may collide with the moored boat after all.

> *"I always feared that the boat would turn over in a strong breeze but found out that it wouldn't— and letting out my mainsail would right me again."*
> **SANDRA HARRISON (40), PALMER, TX**

If you are steering, you may not be totally at fault. When the crew doesn't get the jib trimmed in on the new tack fast enough, the mainsail may force the boat up into the wind again if its sheet remains cleated. By this time the boat has lost so much forward momentum you end up in irons once more.

While the main does not regularly need to be uncleated when tacking, as we said earlier, someone (even the person steering) should hold the mainsheet when sailing among moored boats or near obstructions. If a gust of wind hits the boat, or the tack is not completed well (as described above), you can then release the mainsheet quickly to spill wind out of the main. This lets the boat straighten up so you can change course. In a lot of wind, you will surely be heeled over, making it more difficult to maintain your course or turn away from the wind and away from another boat or object, unless the mainsheet is released.

ANOTHER MUST-KNOW KNOT

A bowline.

Steps for tying a bowline.

One of the most useful knots is the *bowline* (pronounced *bolin*). As a nonslip knot for towing, docking, and a multitude of other purposes, the bowline's major attribute is that no matter how great the strain, the knot won't jam and can easily be untied—unlike many knots that become impossible to loosen when strain is applied.

There are many ways to learn this knot, but the time-honored method is to pretend the end of the line is a rabbit coming out of a hole (the loop) in step 1. Then the rabbit runs around a tree (the standing part of the line) in step 2, and goes back down the hole in step 3. The object is to get the rabbit at the end of the line back through the loop parallel to the way it came out. When you can tie this one in pitch darkness, on a heaving deck, with one hand, you're an old salt!

TEST YOURSELF

On a Tack
Look at the accompanying photo (*right*) to answer the questions below.

1. What tack is this boat on?
2. What side of the boat is the boom over?
3. Where is the wind coming from?

Cycling through the Points of Sail
Look at the accompanying photos and answer the questions below.

1. What point of sail is depicted in each of the five scenarios pictured?
2. Describe the no-go zone and what happens when a boat sails into it.
3. What is sailing by the lee?
4. What are the commands for tacking? For jibing?

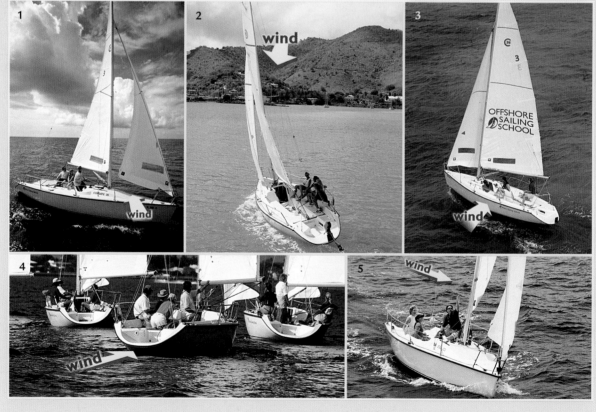

④ WIND AND SAILS
A POWERFUL TEAM

In recent years, a great deal has been learned about the relationship between wind and sails. For a long time sailors thought wind simply pushed sails. When sailing toward the wind, the wind's force is sideways; but the theory was that the wedge shape of the keel kept the boat moving forward. Though not entirely accurate, that theory isn't too far off. Wind exerts both a sideways force and a forward pull on sails. In simplest terms, the keel keeps the boat from slipping sideways—so all that is left is the forward pull.

WIND CREATES LIFT

Forward pull on a sail is caused by air flowing over its surface. To understand this concept, compare your sails to the wings of an airplane. Lift is required to keep a plane in the air, and lift is required to keep a sailboat moving forward.

On an airplane, air splits and passes on either side of its wings. The air on the upper side of a wing has greater velocity than the air on the lower side—because of the *angle of attack* and an airflow phenomenon called *circulation effect*. The angle of attack is defined as the angle between the *chord* (a line from the leading edge to the trailing edge) of an airfoil, and a line representing the undisturbed relative airflow. The circulation effect causes a circular flow that affects velocity and reinforces and accelerates airflow on the upper side of the wing (the leeward side of the sail), while the velocity of flow over the under side of the wing (the windward side of the sail) is opposed and decreased.

Unlike an airplane's wing, all lifting surfaces of a sailboat—the keel, hull, centerboard, and rudder—are symmetrical. Yet they can still develop lift because water hits them at an angle. As air flows past a sail, the sail's curve causes the flow to bend. On the back side of the sail—the leeward side—this results in a greater distance for the wind to travel. In 1738, Daniel Bernoulli discovered that as velocity increases pressure decreases, creating a lift that acts at right angles to the surface. When velocity on both sides of

> *"Learning to sail was a father-son venture. Although we have had wonderful times together, this was an epiphany for me. Sailing is truly a team effort and it is clear that we bonded well as a team."*
>
> **JOHN HESS (61)**
> **AND BILL HILL (28),**
> **OWENSBORO, KY**

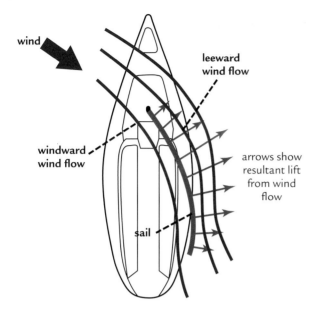

Figure 4-1. Airflow over sails creates lift—Bernoulli's Principle.

the sail and the difference in velocity between the sides of the sail both increase, so does lift.

Deflection of flow is an action that causes an equal and opposite reaction according to Newton's third law of motion. Do you remember, as a child, what happened when you stuck your hand out a car window and then tilted it upward? Because of this deflection and circulation flow, a flat surface or even a thin membrane such as a sail can create lift.

The air, however, has to flow over the surface smoothly and evenly. Once the air starts to separate from the surface it becomes turbulent. Instead of even flow, burbles develop that reduce suction. Much of the turbulence is caused by the angle that the airfoil makes with the airflow. This too is called the *angle of attack* or *angle of incidence*.

If the angle is small, the airflow remains *attached* to the surface for quite a distance back toward the leech of the sail, or the trailing edge of an airplane's wing. When the angle is increased, the airflow detaches earlier and turbulence starts to occur in the forward part of the sail. At a certain angle and speed there is so much separation of flow that the wing or sail no longer develops enough *lift* and a stall occurs. In an airplane the result is dramatic, since the aircraft drops suddenly. A sailboat, however, will just heel over more and slow down.

A sail stalls if it is trimmed in too tight. But a stalled sail can look the same as a sail operating at maximum efficiency. You can easily learn to trim sails properly, by easing them to the point just before they luff. A

luff is easy to see because the leading edge of the sail flaps or flutters. So when trimming your sails, follow this basic rule: ease the sail until it luffs, then trim it just enough to stop the luff.

Like everything else in this world, there are some exceptions. After you have sailed for a while you may find, especially on reaches, the need to trim a little past this point to get maximum drive from the sail. This judgment depends a great deal on wind strength. In lighter winds you can trim tighter before separation and turbulence occur. But the tighter you trim, the more sideways the driving force will be; this can result in detrimental heeling rather than greater forward motion.

TWO SAILS ARE MORE EFFICIENT THAN ONE

Boats with jibs have added advantages over those without. First, the jib is a very efficient sail since there is no

Figure 4-2. The slot between the jib and mainsail improves the wind flow and increases boat speed.

mast in front of it to disrupt airflow. Second, it bends and funnels the air on the leeward side of the main. This funneling action increases the speed of air flowing past the lee side of the main.

The space, or *slot,* between the jib and the mainsail affects the efficiency of airflow when your sails are set properly. The jib not only speeds up this air, but also bends it aft so it can easily follow the curve of the main. Remember, the faster air travels, the less it can bend around the sail. The velocity is substantially faster in the slot between the main and jib, increasing suction and making the mainsail more efficient than it would be without the jib.

> *"Handling the sails and understanding how the wind moves the boat . . . was much easier than we expected."*
>
> **TIM GAPEN (56), WISCONSIN RAPIDS, WI**

With an accurate handheld windspeed indicator, you can measure the difference in the velocity of airflow on the lee side of the mainsail with and without a jib. You can also feel wind velocity without any instruments. When you are sailing close-hauled, before you unfurl the jib, crouch under the boom with arms on either side of the mainsail, as if you are surrendering. Then ask someone to unroll the jib and trim it in. You will immediately feel more wind pressure on the leeward side of the main than on the windward side.

Without a jib, the efficiency of the mainsail is greatly reduced. Air is not funneled along the main, flow becomes detached, and turbulence occurs. Remember that attached airflow creates lift. When sailing close-hauled, it is important to keep the slot open. For example, if you ease the main before easing the jib, you can close this slot and create *backwind* on the mainsail. Although the main looks like it is luffing, the air is no longer flowing smoothly through the slot. Always make sure the jib is properly trimmed be-

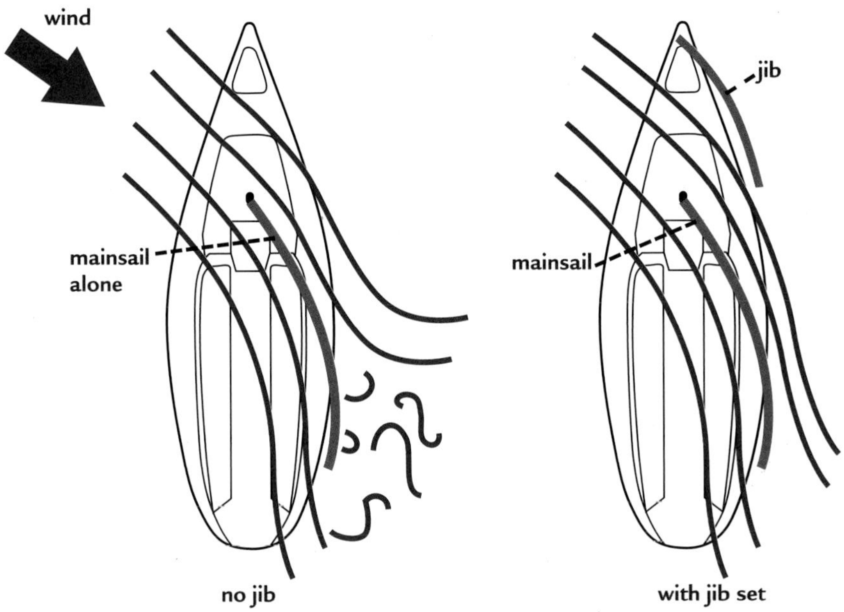

Figure 4-3. Airflow detaches early and turbulence occurs when there is no jib. When the jib is set, air flows across the width of the mainsail and creates better lift.

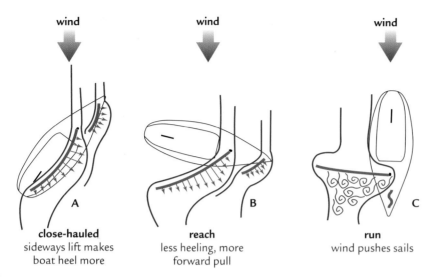

close-hauled
sideways lift makes
boat heel more

reach
less heeling, more
forward pull

run
wind pushes sails

Figure 4-4. How lift affects heeling.

fore adjusting the mainsail. As you can now understand, a boat can sail with just a mainsail or jib; but the combination of main and jib makes your sails more efficient.

THE EFFECT OF HEELING

Heeling is a mixed bag for sailors. Until you learn why a boat heels, you might feel uncomfortable with the sensation of being at an angle to the horizon. Some macho, experienced sailors love the challenge of sailing with the rail in the water. But for many reasons, which we'll cover later, that is not a very efficient way to sail.

When a boat is close-hauled with sails trimmed in tight, a large sideways push on the sails makes your boat heel. In Figure 4-4, note that many of the force arrows point sideways on Boat A, which is sailing close-hauled. As the sail is eased out to a reach (Boat B) the arrows start to line up more with the course of the boat, which results in less heeling and more forward pull. A reach, therefore, is usually the fastest point of sailing.

It may appear that you're sailing faster when you are close-hauled because there's a great deal of commotion, the boat is heeling over and plowing through the seas, and the wind seems stronger because you are moving toward it. When you fall off to a reach, however, the commotion quiets down. You are sailing across the wind and water and neither seem to be as powerful. The boat is more upright because the pull of the sails is more forward.

Carrying this one step further, you might think that a run would be even faster because the wind and the boat are both going in the same direction. But on a run, the wind is just pushing the boat and can't flow over both sides of the sail. Lift cannot develop on the leeward side of the sail, and (as you see in Boat C), there is pure turbulence behind the sail downwind. If a jib is set on this point of sail, no wind can reach it because the main is blocking the wind from reaching the jib; in this case, the jib is *blanketed* by the main.

Again, there can be exceptions. When the wind velocity increases to the point where a boat on a reach is *overpowered* and heeling excessively in comparison to forward drive, a run can then be the faster point of sail.

USING TELLTALES

To sail efficiently, you need to maintain the optimum drive angle of the wind on your sails. You can do this by steering well and trimming your sails properly. To help visualize proper sail trim, imagine air flowing past your sails as smoke. Many wind tunnel tests, called *smoke visualization tests*, actually use smoke to see the difference between smooth and turbulent flow. Obviously you can't create a smokescreen in front of your sailboat, but you can do the next best thing: attach telltales to the sails to show whether the flow past the sail is turbulent or smooth. Normally, these telltales are attached at three levels on the jib.

On the boat in Figure 4-5 you can see three sets of telltales on the jib and another set on each shroud. You have already learned that telltales are placed on the shrouds to show *wind direction*. The telltales on your sail show *wind flow* on the leeward and windward sides of the sail.

These telltales on your sail are like a mine canary. They warn you when you are about to lose your jib's efficiency before you can actually see the sail flutter. When the telltale on one side of the sail isn't flowing nicely aft, that telltale is telling you airflow is disrupted. But when the telltales on both the leeward and windward side of the sail stream aft, airflow is smooth and even.

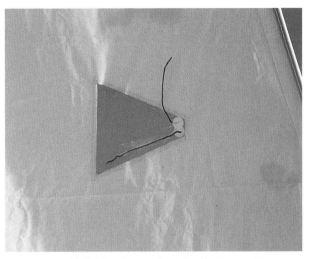

Figure 4-6. Telltales show when the jib is eased too much. This windward telltale (green here) is fluttering.

Figure 4-5. Telltales on the sail help you see airflow. Telltales on the shrouds help you see wind direction.

On the sail in Figure 4-6, the windward telltale is pointing up and the leeward telltale is flowing aft. Airflow on the windward side of the sail is not smooth. Either the jib is eased too much and needs to be trimmed in, or the person steering is *pinching*—sailing too high and too close to the wind. When the windward telltale is flowing properly and the leeward telltale is fluttering, the jib is trimmed too tight or the person steering is sailing too far off the wind (too low).

When steering close-hauled, watch the telltales and keep them in line by moving the tiller slightly until you get the desired results. If you are sailing on a reach, the crew should make subtle adjustments to the jib (ease out slightly, pull in a little) until both telltales are streaming aft. Telltales on the mainsail, placed on the leech end of batten pockets, are not important for

Figure 4-7. When both telltales stream aft, airflow is smooth and even.

recreational sailing. Racing sailors, however, do use them.

You can test how well you are steering or how well the sails are trimmed in a couple of simple exercises. Watch the middle set of telltales on the jib as you change your heading without varying your jib trim. As the boat heads up toward the wind, the windward telltale starts to flutter. Conversely, when the boat heads too far off the wind, the leeward telltale flutters because the angle of attack becomes so great the wind hits

TILLER TOWARD FLUTTERING TELLTALE

- Leeward telltale flutters, sailing too low
- Windward telltale flutters, sailing too high

"We had an amazing experience. My husband and I had very little experience on the water and we walked away from the Offshore Sailing course confident in our new-found skills. A week later we purchased a Catalina 25 and we could not be happier. Thank you for starting us out the correct way— you should see us folding our mainsail 'just so.'"

JENNY BRITT (34), SEA CLIFF, NY

mostly on the windward side of the sail. This disrupts flow over the lee side and turbulence results.

If turbulence occurs on the lee side, the jib stalls and no longer produces the desired drive. As explained earlier, an impending luff is easy to see because the sail starts to flutter along the luff; but a stall is virtually invisible. So, ease the jib until the windward telltales start to flutter; then trim again until telltales on both sides of the jib stream aft. The difference between a luff and a stall is usually no more than a slight (5°–10°) change in heading.

Telltales are very helpful for the new sailor, and they are also used to advantage by the expert. Dr. Reinhorn, a 1967 Offshore Sailing School graduate, came up with a simple rule for steering to windward that we have used ever since. Dubbed Reinhorn's Law, this little phrase will always keep you out of trouble: *Point the tiller at the fluttering telltale.*

For example, if the leeward telltale is fluttering you are sailing too low, too far away from the wind for the desired close-hauled course. You need to point closer to the wind, so move the tiller to leeward to cure this. If the windward telltale is fluttering, you are sailing too close to the wind and you are on the verge of a luff. To solve this problem, move the tiller to windward and the boat will fall off. As you move the tiller, make slight course adjustments. It doesn't take much to get those telltales streaming together again.

When trying to reach a destination, use your telltales to find the fastest way to get there. If you are on course, adjust the jib (pull in or ease out) to make the telltales stream aft together. If you are sailing close-hauled and can't trim the sails any tighter, steer the boat to make the telltales stream aft.

As usual, there are exceptions when telltales should not be flowing on both sides. In a strong wind and smooth sea you may be able to *pinch* (carry a very slight luff in the jib) and still maintain your speed or even go faster. In this case it is okay for the windward telltale to flutter. If you fall off until both sides flow evenly, the boat will heel a lot, reducing your speed. Experienced sailors steer the fastest course for existing conditions.

Jib telltales help you gain speed on a reach, but you need to *play* (trim and ease) the jib constantly to use them effectively. This means easing when the jib stalls and trimming when it luffs. Racing crew keep their eyes glued to the telltales near the luff of the sail, with the jibsheet in hand—whether they are sailing on a small boat or on a large yacht. Without those telltales on the jib, it is very, very difficult to determine if the sail is stalled.

WIND FLOW ON A RUN

When a reach becomes very broad and approaches a run, the force of the wind changes from a *pull* to a *push*. Instead of flow over the lee side of the sail you end up with *drag* (the force that slows movement of the boat through the air or water). The sail that creates the most drag will push the boat fastest. Though you want to retain aerodynamic flow over the lee side as long as possible, at some point near a run the curve of the sail is no longer helpful and the amount of sail area exposed to the wind is now the most important factor.

Just as a large parachute will lower you more gently than a small one, a large sail will push the boat faster than a small one downwind. As you reach the point where sail area projected to the wind is more important, the leeward telltales (which were flowing aft) start to flutter and easing the sail more doesn't seem to help much. In fact, it will hurt your speed because you start to lose sail area. In practicality, if your boat is rigged to carry a spinnaker (a large parachute-looking sail), you would have probably set one before you reach this point. If you only have a jib and no spinnaker, you might *wing* your jib out to the other side of the boat.

When you sail *wing and wing*, you sail downwind with the mainsail on one side and the jib on the other. This helps move the boat more efficiently downwind because you are exposing more sail area. Sometimes you can just hold the jib out over the side opposite the mainsail. Other times you may want to rig a pole from the clew of the sail back to the mast. When sailing wing and wing with a pole, you will lose one of your early-warning signals for an accidental jibe. The jib may want to move across from one side to the other, but the pole won't let it; you could be on the verge of an accidental jibe, so you need to keep a close eye on the wind direction and your boom.

In Figure 4-9, the jib on the second boat cannot fill because it is blanketed behind its mainsail. The lead boat is sailing more efficiently, with the jib winged out on the side opposite of the main where it can catch more wind.

JIB LEADS

Telltales are also an important aid when determining how jibsheets should lead from the clew of the sail to a winch in the cockpit. On almost all sailboats, jibsheets are led through blocks on tracks on the starboard and port sides of the deck. These adjustable leads determine the shape of the jib. When the block is too far forward, the foot of the jib is too loose and the leech is too tight, because most of the pull on the jib sheet is downward. When the block is too far aft, the foot is stretched too tight and the leech is too loose because of the backward pull.

What you want is a compromise between the two extremes to avoid distorting the sail. There should be an even flow of air on both sides of the sail at all levels along the luff. If

Figure 4-8. Sailing wing and wing with jib and main on opposite sides of the boat.

Figure 4-9. The jib on the boat behind is blanketed by its main, while the lead boat sails wing and wing.

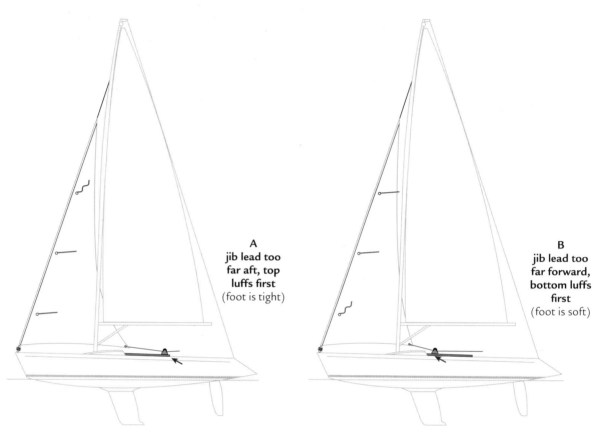

A
jib lead too
far aft, top
luffs first
(foot is tight)

B
jib lead too
far forward,
bottom luffs
first
(foot is soft)

Figure 4-10. How jib leads affect flow at top and bottom of the sail. A. If top of jib luffs first, move jib lead forward. B. If bottom of jib luffs first, move jib lead aft.

the lead is too far forward, the bottom of the sail will have a big curve in it and the lower part of the sail will luff first. Conversely, if the lead is too far aft, the leech will be loose and tend to fall off at the top of the sail, causing that part to luff first. So the test to determine proper jib lead placement is to head the boat up slowly until the jib begins to luff. If it luffs at the top first, the lead is too far aft. If it luffs at the bottom first, the lead is too far forward. But if it luffs the full length of the sail all at the same time, the lead is set in the right spot.

Telltales also allow you to determine if any part of your jib is stalled. If the bottom leeward telltale flutters first, the bottom of the sail is stalled. The sail is too flat at the bottom because the jib lead is too far aft.

HOW SAILS ARE MADE

Sails are your sailboat's engine, their driving force. The shape of your sails allows you to change gears and throttling power. Full sails are like low gear in a car; flat sails are like high gear. Full sails can be likened to flaps down on an airplane, giving power to get up into the air. At cruising altitude, pilots bring the flaps back in to maintain speed going forward. You will adjust sails in much the same way.

TESTING PROPER JIB LEADS

- ◆ Head up slowly until the jib begins to luff
- ◆ If the jib luffs at the top first, the lead is too far aft
- ◆ If the jib luffs at bottom first, the lead is too far forward
- ◆ If the jib luffs along full length of the sail, the leads are set correctly

Figure 4-11. Chord, camber, and draft define sail shape.

SAIL POWER

- Full sails—deep draft, more power through water, cause boat to heel more
- Flat sails—shallow draft, less powerful, boat heels less

The distance from luff to leech in a straight line at any level in the sail is the chord. If three people, one at each corner, pick up a sail lying flat on the ground, a belly will form as they hold it level. This belly is called the *camber*. The distance from the deepest point of the camber to the chord is the *draft*.

A deep draft sail is considered a *full* sail and is used like first gear in a car—for slow speeds (light winds) and for power in choppy seas (similar to climbing a steep hill). A shallow-draft sail is called a *flat* sail and is used like high gear in a car—not much power but appropriate for high winds and flat seas.

The threads that run across a strip of sailcoth are called *filling threads*, otherwise known as the *weft* or the *fill*. The threads that run lengthwise are

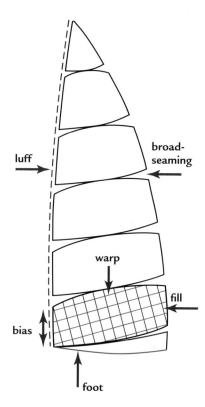

Figure 4-12. Warp, fill, and bias define how sail cloth stretches.

called the *warp*. Warp stretches more than fill, but the greatest stretch comes in a diagonal direction, called the *bias*.

Most sails are designed with this stretch in mind. The mainsheet will exert the greatest force on a mainsail and most of it will fall on the leech. Consequently, the panels of cloth are sewn together so the crosswise threads, or filling threads, lie parallel to the leech of the sail. Thus all the panels of the luff along the mast, where stretch is greatest, are cut on the bias. If you could blow up a small section of the sail along the mast, you would see that the threads look like a whole bunch of little diamonds on the bias. As you pull down on the luff and increase the tension, each diamond elongates and pulls material in from the center of the sail.

As a result, if you pull down hard on the luff when there isn't enough wind, vertical creases will appear that run parallel to the mast. You can simulate this effect by taking a handkerchief and pulling it at two diagonally opposite corners. The same creases will appear just as they will when there is too much tension on a sail. Note that the panels are curved. When the panels are sewn together by the sailmaker, a curve, which allows for draft, is created in the sail. This process is called *broadseaming*.

There is a hole in the luff of the mainsail a foot or so above the tack with a line running through it. Strengthened by a metal grommet, this assembly has become known as the *cunningham* and is now commonplace on most sailboats. In heavy winds, sailcloth can stretch and the sail becomes full just when you want it to be flat. Pulling down on the cunningham moves the draft forward in the sail and cures this effect. Some wrinkles will appear along the tack below the grommet when the cunningham is in use, but they don't seem to make an appreciable difference in the efficiency of the sail, so ignore them.

SAIL CONTROLS

As the velocity of the wind increases or decreases, you need to adjust the draft of your sails for the best efficiency. For instance, you set sail in a 10-knot wind and the shape of your sails looks good. Soon the wind increases to 20 knots and now you are overpowered. With older Dacron sails, the draft of your mainsail may have moved aft with stretch. The leech of the mainsail is tight and becomes a rudder in the air, steering you to windward. So, you need to flatten your sails and bring the draft of your mainsail back to its original position. The *outhaul* stretches and flattens the lower part of the mainsail along the boom. The *backstay* bends the mast forward in the middle when tightened. This frees the leech, reduces weather helm, and makes a flatter sail. The *cunningham* tightens the lower luff of the sail, which keeps the draft forward. The halyard stretches the whole luff, particularly higher up.

"Sail trim and shape were difficult concepts to grasp at first, but they proved to be worthwhile lessons. We soon realized there's a better, faster way to sail."
JON NELSON (50), DOWNINGTOWN, PA

Figure 4-13. A. Sail controls that adjust draft and ultimately sail shape. B. Terms that define a sail's shape.

Mainsheet tension pulls the end of the boom down, tightens the leech, increases draft, and increases weather helm. Be careful in light air about trimming the mainsail too tight. Remember: *when in doubt, let it out.*

The *traveler* and *boom vang* also control tension along the leech of the sail. The traveler is a track that's mounted behind the cockpit (sometimes behind the tiller, sometimes in front). A sliding block with a part of the mainsheet reeved through it runs along the traveler and allows you to change the mainsail's angle to the wind. The boom vang is an angled block and tackle arrangement or adjustable rod that runs from a tang or block on the boom to another fitting near the base of the mast or to a rail on the side of the boat. The boom vang keeps the boom from rising and keeps the leech tight. A tight leech cocks to windward and causes a full sail because the chord line moves away from the belly of the sail, increasing the draft as shown as solid lines in the diagram (Figure 4-13B). A loose leech falls off to leeward and flattens the sail (dotted lines).

READING AND USING THE WIND

For the best efficiency, you'll need to adjust your sails according to your boat's precise angle to the wind. However, wind is constantly changing direction, so sails require constant fine tuning.

Before you go sailing, check weather maps in local newspapers, the forecasts put out by the National Oceanic and Atmospheric Administration (NOAA), or any other source that gives you some credible wind and weather predictions. Remember that local topography and large buildings can bend and deflect the wind, so you need to take this into consideration when you hear reports of wind direction and strength.

You cannot see the wind, but you can see how it affects the surface of the water. So as you sail, watch the water all around you. You will see *puffs*, or gusts of wind, which indicate greater wind velocity; these move across the water in patches of ripples. The ripples also show you where a new wind is coming from, especially on a light-air day. If you are sailing close-hauled on starboard tack and see ripples approaching from abeam, you should anticipate a new wind direction, which may be temporary. *Lulls* indicate reduced wind velocity and manifest themselves as smoother areas on the water. As puffs move and lulls form, you can detect changes in wind direction and strength.

"I love the challenge of making a boat go by working with nature. It's calming and invigorating at the same time. One must stay focused on the wind and the water to keep going.... It's amazing how an activity can be so relaxing yet can require so much attention. I really believe one's understanding and awe of nature and our universe is heightened by sailing and wish everyone could have this experience. Hearing the wind and the water all around my boat and knowing I can use it to get someplace is nirvana to me."

LEANN SMITH (46), KANSAS CITY, MO

Headers and Lifts

Sailors talk about *true wind* and *apparent wind*. True wind is the actual wind. Apparent wind is the wind you feel as the boat moves,

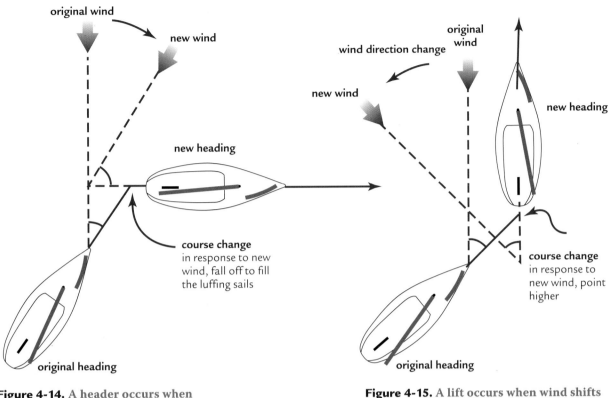

Figure 4-14. A header occurs when wind shifts toward the bow.

Figure 4-15. A lift occurs when wind shifts toward the stern.

described later in this chapter. A shift of true wind direction is called a *header* or a *lift*, depending on the relationship of the shift to the heading of the boat.

When the wind shifts more toward the bow of your boat, this shift is called a *header*. If you are sailing close-hauled, the sails will luff, necessitating a change of course away from the wind to keep them filled. You would say the boat has been *headed* or has *sailed into a header*. When the wind shifts more toward the stern of your boat, allowing you to *steer higher* than before, the boat has been *lifted* or is sailing *in a lift*.

When a header or a lift occurs on a reach, a corresponding sail adjustment is required to maintain your course. So on a reach, trim for a header, ease for a lift. A wind shift that is a header for a boat on port tack is a lift for a boat on starboard

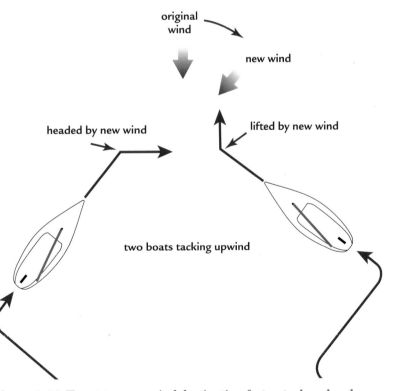

Figure 4-16. To get to an upwind destination faster, tack on headers.

Figure 4-17. A backing wind heads this boat while a veering wind is a lift.

TRUE WIND

- Changes strength—puffs (gusts) and lulls
- Changes direction—veers (clockwise), backs (counterclockwise)
- Header—true wind moves toward bow
- Lift—true wind moves toward stern

tack. A boat sailing on a lift will reach its desired upwind destination faster than one sailing in a header, since the lifted boat can sail a closer course to its upwind destination. So if you are headed and want to continue sailing upwind toward your destination in the shortest distance possible, you should tack.

When a wind shift is described in relation to the course you are sailing, it's described as a *header* or a *lift*. But when a wind shift is described in relation to a compass direction, it is said to be *veering* or *backing*.

Wind that shifts clockwise—from north to northeast, for example—is *veering*. Wind that shifts counterclockwise—from east to northeast, for example—is *backing*. A north wind is one that blows *from* the north. (Don't confuse these with currents, which are named for the direction to which they flow. For instance, a current that comes from the south, flowing northward, is a northerly current.)

Wind shifts are changes in the direction of the actual (true) wind blowing over the water. Picture yourself steering the boat in Figure 4-17. Your destination is roughly in the middle of the shoreline. If the wind veers (shifts clockwise), you will be in a lift; you'll then be able to point higher and sail closer toward your destination on land without tacking. If the wind backs (shifts counterclockwise), you will be headed; you'll then end up sailing at a broad angle away from your destination. But if you tack, you might be headed directly home.

Apparent Wind

Another type of shift, which also causes the need for sail adjustment, is a change in the *apparent* wind direction. While true wind is what your masthead fly and telltales show when your boat is not moving through the water (at anchor or docked), apparent wind is what you *feel* and what you see in your telltales and masthead fly when the boat is underway.

Apparent wind is derived from the combination of wind produced by the boat moving through the air and wind produced by nature (true wind). Cigarette smoke, telltales, and electronic wind-direction indicators all indicate apparent wind direction when you are moving.

Imagine that you are standing up in a convertible on a windless day. As the convertible starts forward, you begin to feel a breeze on your face that increases as the speed of the car increases. This is like boat speed wind. At 10 mph, you feel a 10-mph breeze on your face. This is *apparent* wind.

Now imagine yourself in the same parked car, pointing north with an easterly wind (true wind) of 10 mph. You feel that wind hitting the right side of your face. As the car starts forward you don't feel two different winds—one on the side and one on the front of your face. You feel a resultant wind coming from an angle forward of the true wind. This is *apparent* wind.

Figure 4-18 shows apparent wind when towing a boat at 6 knots on a dead-calm day. Since there is no true wind, a resultant angle is not produced and the apparent wind is coming from dead ahead at the same

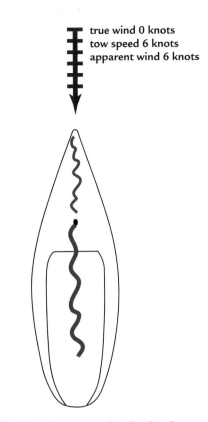

Figure 4-18. Towing a boat on a dead-calm day creates apparent wind dead ahead.

speed as the boat: 6 knots. On your first day out on a close-hauled course, you may wonder why the telltales on the shrouds indicate you are almost sailing directly into the wind, while you are technically sailing around 45° off the wind. The telltales are indicating your apparent wind—the resultant angle of your boat's forward motion and the true wind.

You can demonstrate the force and direction of apparent wind by drawing a parallelogram on graph paper, keeping your boat's speed and the true wind in the same scale. Figure 4-19 shows a boat close-hauled, sailing at 6 knots in a 12-knot true wind. Suppose you know your boat tacks in an 80° arc (the distance it will travel when moving from one tack to another). Therefore, the true wind direction is at half of your tacking range, or 40° off your bow. To find the strength and direction of the wind you feel—the apparent wind—draw a parallelogram on the graph paper using your boat speed (6 knots) and the true wind (12 knots). Then draw a diagonal line through the parallelogram. The diagonal line measures 17 knots of apparent wind by your scale. Now, using a protractor, the apparent wind reads 27° from your heading (versus 40° for the true wind).

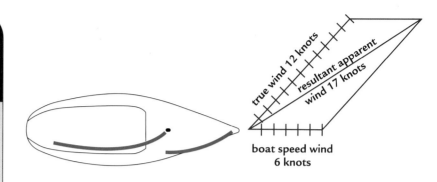

APPARENT WIND DOWNWIND

♦ Apparent wind is *less* than true wind.
♦ Wind coming from behind feels like the wind has died—because true wind and boat speed counteract each other.
♦ When changing course, apparent wind can swing wildly.
♦ A boat is sometimes sailing by the lee—apparent wind is on the same side of boat as the boom.
♦ Beware of an accidental jibe.

Figure 4-19. **When close-hauled, apparent wind is both stronger and more forward of true wind.**

This demonstrates that on a close-hauled course, the apparent wind is greater than true wind strength.

There are four points to remember about apparent wind:

1. The strength of apparent wind lessens as true wind comes aft.
2. Apparent wind is always forward of true wind, unless true wind is dead ahead or astern.
3. When true wind is well aft, a small change in true wind direction makes a large change in apparent wind direction.
4. When on a beam reach or close-hauled, apparent wind is of greater velocity than true wind.

The first point states that as true wind comes aft, the apparent wind speed lessens. This is obvious if you have ever seen powerboats head directly downwind. Sometimes they cruise along at the same speed and direction as the true wind. This is when apparent wind and true wind line up and cancel each other out. Their engine exhaust hangs around the boat in an enveloping cloud, and the apparent wind is just about zero (yet another reason why sailing is so much more fun!).

On a reach, as you can see in Figure 4-20, the wind speed lessens—even though the boat speed wind and true wind are pretty much the same as when you were close-hauled. The decrease in wind speed you feel on the boat can lull you into forgetting that the wind will be stronger when you change direction and head up to a beat. You may have started sailing on a run and had no idea what the apparent wind strength would be on a beat. Or the wind may have increased during the run. Either way, if the wind is blowing hard, you must consider the possibility that you may want less sail area when you go to a close-hauled course.

The second point states that apparent wind is always forward of

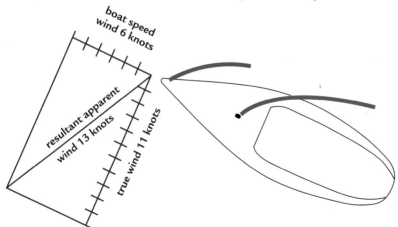

Figure 4-20. **On a reach the apparent wind is less than when close-hauled. Compare this diagram with Figure 4-19.**

true wind, unless true wind is dead ahead or astern. This is important when you are sailing downwind and need to consider when to jibe. For better speed, it is desirable to sail at a slight angle to the wind rather than dead (directly) downwind; but this means you may have to jibe to reach your destination. It is therefore important to determine the direction of the true wind and the angle your heading is making with it.

For example, if you know you are steering 20° from dead downwind on one tack, then you will be on the same point of sail when you are 20° from dead downwind on the other tack. The right time to jibe is when your destination bears 40° off your bow from your present heading. To find the true wind direction, head off momentarily until you are dead downwind, allowing the apparent wind and true wind to line up. The difference between the new heading and your former heading (20° in the example above; 40° when doubled) is the number of degrees in which you will jibe (Figure 4-21).

In Figure 4-22, your boat is going 6 knots in a 12-knot breeze. If you are sailing dead downwind, the apparent wind is true wind minus boat speed, or just 6 knots. This doesn't feel like much wind, and the force on your sails is relatively light. But when you start beating at 6 knots, the apparent wind increases to almost 17 knots.

You might assume that since the apparent wind is now about three times greater than the downwind velocity, it exerts three times as much force against the sails. But that assumption would be wrong. The force of the wind *quadruples* as the velocity doubles (the square of the velocity), so the wind force is *nine times greater* on a close-hauled course than on a run in this case. Couple this with a lot of heeling, and the boat may very well be overpowered. The lesson here is to consider shortening sail before you turn to go upwind.

The third point states that when true wind is well aft, a small change in the true wind direction makes a large change in apparent wind direction. This is one factor, among others, that makes steering dead downwind so dif-

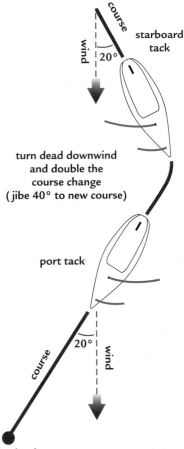

Figure 4-21. How to determine new course after jibing.

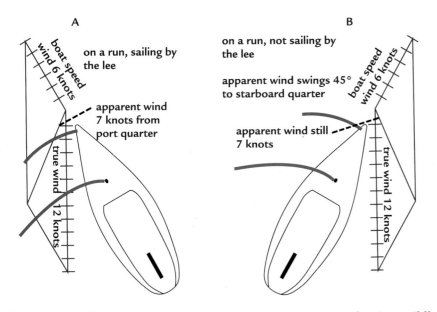

Figure 4-22. When changing course downwind, apparent wind swings wildly.

Figure 4-23. Sailing by the lee, with the wind on the same side as the boom, this boat is in danger of jibing.

ficult. If you have a lot of wave action when steering downwind, the boat's stern and rudder can be pushed to one side or the other by the waves. This complicates staying on course because you must anticipate wave action as well as wind shifts.

If your stern is pushed by a wave, the effect is the same as a change in wind direction. When the wind gets on the same side as the boom (by the lee) because of either wave action or a wind shift, you are in danger of a jibe. As you try to get back on course, wind direction swings from one side of the boat to the other. Inexperienced sailors tend to oversteer in this situation, causing repetitive swings (oscillation), because they are late in compensating for the turn of the boat and often move the tiller too far.

In Figure 4-23, the lead boat is sailing by the lee. In this case, the wind is on the same side as the boom and the mainsail looks like it might accidentally jibe. The first sign of an accidental jibe is when the jib starts to come across. When this occurs, heed the instructor's warning: *Turn tiller to boom to avoid doom.* Another sign of that doom is when the shroud telltales on the windward side point away from the boat.

The last point about apparent wind states that when a boat is reaching or beating, the apparent wind is of greater velocity than the true wind. This means you are, in effect, making your own wind. For example, ice boats can attain very high speeds; some easily reach speeds that are five to six times the speed of the wind, because they experience very little surface friction. Boat speeds of 120 knots in 24 knots of wind are not unusual!

The faster the boat goes, the higher the wind velocity it creates. But a normal sailboat is limited in speed by hull resistance, skin friction, and wave-making drag—so it cannot take full advantage of the increased apparent wind velocity. Even so, the faster a boat is to windward, the more *close-winded* (able to sail close to the wind) it will be.

Lulls and Puffs

As you sail along you may suddenly feel a dramatic drop in wind strength. You have sailed into a *lull,* and the apparent wind has gone forward and decreased because your boat speed is now a greater factor than the wind speed, until the boat slows down. Conversely, you might also see a *puff,* a big patch of ripples, approaching you; the apparent wind moves aft and increases, and you suddenly feel a strong increase in wind strength because the wind speed is a greater factor than boat speed.

In Figures 4-19, 4-20, and 4-22, everything remained constant except the direction of the true wind, which moved farther aft in each subsequent diagram. What happens if you change wind velocity, keeping the true wind direction at 45° off the bow?

In Figure 4-24, initially the wind speed was 10 knots and the boat speed was 4 knots. The extension of the true wind line indicates a *puff* with a 4-knot increase. The apparent wind moves aft as the puff hits; but by the time your boat picks up speed, the puff has usually passed.

When a puff is very strong, it causes your boat to heel dramatically if you don't make any adjustments. To reduce heeling when hit by a powerful gust, point the boat higher toward the wind. As the gust hits, apparent wind goes aft, causing more heeling and less drive. This changes the angle of attack—the angle the apparent wind makes with the sails. Now your sails are improperly trimmed until you head up or ease sheets or the traveler.

This change in apparent wind direction is important to remember even on light days. On days when you have a 3-knot breeze, the wind velocity in a puff is apt to be more than double the regular breeze. When it is blowing 15 knots, gusts may get to only 20 to 22 knots—or about a third higher. Thus, the change in apparent wind direction aft is often greater on light days than on heavy ones. But if the wind dies suddenly, apparent wind goes forward. In Figure 4-24, boat speed remains constant; when the wind velocity lowers to 6 knots, the apparent wind goes forward.

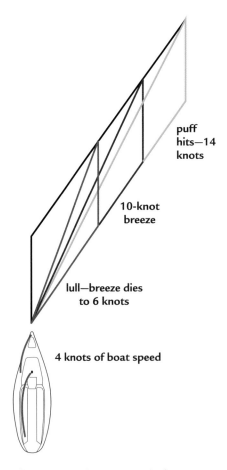

puff hits—14 knots

10-knot breeze

lull—breeze dies to 6 knots

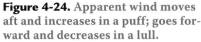

4 knots of boat speed

Figure 4-24. Apparent wind moves aft and increases in a puff; goes forward and decreases in a lull.

LULLS AND PUFFS

- In a lull, apparent wind goes forward and decreases.
- In a puff, apparent wind goes aft and increases.

TEST YOURSELF

Telltales and Sail Trim

Picture yourself sailing the boat in the accompanying photo.

1. What point of sail are you on?
2. If the windward telltale flutters, should you ease or trim the jib?
3. If the leeward telltale flutters, are you steering too low or too high?
4. If you are on course and heading home, do you turn the boat or trim the sails to get there?
5. How does a jib enhance sailing efficiency?
6. What do telltales on the shrouds tell you?
7. What do telltales on the jib tell you?

Sail Controls

1. Find the outhaul, backstay, cunningham, mainsheet traveler, and boom vang on the boat in the accompanying photo.
2. Describe draft in a sail.
3. Does deep draft cause more or less heeling?
4. How does shallow draft affect sail power?

TEST YOURSELF

Wind Shifts and Direction

Answer the questions below on wind shifts and wind direction, based on what you have learned in this chapter.

1. Describe true wind.
2. Explain the difference between veering and backing winds.
3. What is a lift?
4. What is a header?
5. Describe apparent wind.
6. When you are close-hauled, is apparent wind stronger or lighter than true wind?
7. Describe a boat sailing by the lee.
8. How do you know when you are sailing by the lee?

5 BALANCE AND STABILITY

In order to sail properly, and certainly in order to race successfully, you must understand the *balance* and *stability* of your boat. A well-balanced boat will tend to maintain its heading when you release the tiller, and a stable boat can absorb more force of wind in its sails without heeling excessively. The greater the ability of a boat to stay upright, all else being equal, the faster it will go. A stable boat is sometimes called a *powerful* boat.

HOW WEATHER AND LEE HELM AFFECT BALANCE

If you release the tiller and the boat turns away from the wind (to leeward) you are experiencing *lee helm*. Conversely, if the boat turns to windward you are experiencing *weather helm*. If the boat sails straight ahead, it is perfectly balanced. When sailing to windward, however, a little weather helm is desirable, for reasons we'll examine shortly.

There are many reasons for weather or lee helm, but foremost is the relationship between the *center of effort* (CE) of the sails (called, collectively, the *sail plan*) and the *center of lateral resistance* (CLR) of the hull.

Imagine a sailboat viewed in profile—this includes the hull underbody, keel, and rudder. Now imagine balancing the boat on your fingertip. When you find that balance point, you've found the center of lateral resistance, or CLR.

To find the center of effort (CE) of a sloop-rigged sailboat, you would find the geometric center of the jib, and then of the main, and finally the combined geometric center of the two sails together. In practice, the overall CE will be closer to the center of the mainsail than the jib, since the main is usually the larger sail. The CE is the focal point of the wind forces acting to push the boat sideways against the resistance of the hull underbody and underwater appendages, which is focused at the CLR. If you add or move

THE FEEL OF A BOAT

The feel of the boat is affected by:

- Center of lateral resistance (CLR)—the geometric center of all the underwater surfaces of a boat
- Center of effort (CE)—the geometric center of all the sails that are set

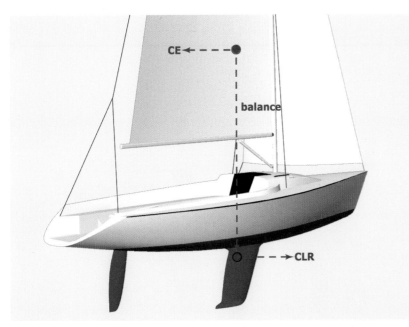

Figure 5-1. When the center of effort (CE) is directly above the center of lateral resistance (CLR), a boat is usually in balance.

CHANGING THE CLR

Although the center of lateral resistance is difficult to change underway, it can be altered by:

◆ Adding weight to immerse the bow more deeply—CLR moves forward
◆ Adding weight to immerse the stern more deeply—CLR moves aft

weight toward the bow, the CLR moves forward. If you add or move weight toward the stern, the CLR moves aft. If you sail a centerboard boat, the CLR moves aft when the board is raised partway (assuming it pivots aft when raised).

Now picture a model sailboat complete with sails, like a weather vane on top of a roof pivoting on its CLR. When the CE is directly above the CLR, the boat is in balance and won't pivot in the wind. However, if you place more sail area toward the bow of the boat, the CE moves forward of the CLR, and the bow of the boat tends to pivot to leeward, away from the wind. If you move the CE behind the CLR by placing more sail area near the stern of the boat, the bow pivots to windward, toward the wind.

HOW SAILS AFFECT BALANCE

The easiest way to change the balance of your boat, at least while sailing, is to move your effective sail area forward or aft. In theory, if you move the mast aft (and with it the main and jib), weather helm increases (CE is aft of CLR). Conversely, if you move the mast and sails forward, weather helm is reduced and a lee helm, if present, increases (CE is forward of CLR). Since most boats have varying amounts of weather helm and rarely have lee helm, the most likely result would be a reduction in weather helm.

In practice, however, moving the whole rig forward or aft is time-consuming on a small boat and close to impossible on a large one without extensive carpentry. An alternative solution is to change either the amount of sail forward or aft or the trim of those sails. The design of the Colgate 26 makes it quite easy to sail, without excessive weather or lee helm, with just the main or jib alone. But on many boats, if you sail without a jib your boat may have strong weather helm produced by the mainsail, and under jib alone

CHANGING THE CENTER OF EFFORT

The center of effort is easy to change underway:

◆ Reduce or add sail area forward or aft
◆ Luff the mainsail to move the CE forward; luff the jib to move it aft
◆ Move or tilt the mast forward or aft

WEATHER HELM

- Weather helm is the tendency of a boat to turn *toward* the wind
- It is caused by a CE that is *aft* of the CLR
- A boat with weather helm *heads up* in gusts, which is what you want it to do
- Weather helm also gives *lift* to the rudder, and this too is good

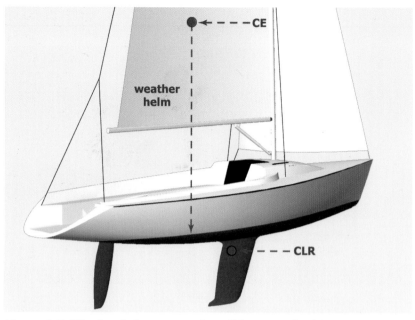

Figure 5-2. Weather helm occurs when CE moves aft of CLR.

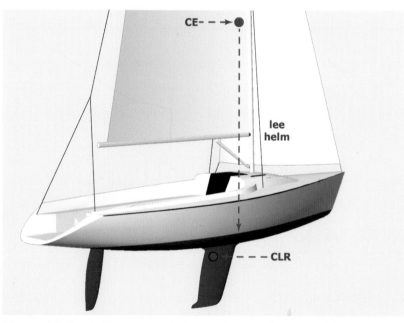

Figure 5-3. Lee helm is caused when CE moves forward of CLR.

the boat may have strong lee helm. In such a case, if you luff the mainsail, you should reduce its efficiency enough to move the CE forward with a corresponding reduction in weather helm. If you luff the jib, the weather helm should increase.

A boat with too much weather helm is harder to turn away from the wind. You may feel it *rounding up* toward the wind in puffs, and in this case you should have someone ready to ease the mainsheet if you are sailing in the vicinity of other boats or having trouble controlling where you want to go.

A boat with lee helm, on the other hand, tries to turn away from the wind. There really are no benefits to having lee helm, and a boat that is constantly trying to turn downwind will get you into trouble sooner or later. A little weather helm, as stated earlier, is best.

If you carefully adjust your main and jib, you can steer a fairly straight course without even touching the tiller. This is good practice—because one never knows when a rudder might fall off or when a tiller might break, as it did for us in the middle of a transatlantic race. With no rudder, we steered the last 1,000 miles just by trimming and easing our sails.

To practice sailing without a rudder on a close-hauled course, trim the jib fairly flat and then play the mainsheet—luffing the main to head off, trimming it to head up. On a reach you can balance the boat by easing the main to reduce weather helm. On a run, ease the main way out and ask a crew member to sit to windward to heel the boat. You may need to take the mainsail down if your boat keeps rounding up, then sail with the jib alone. To tack, ask crew members to move to the leeward side of the boat, then luff the jib completely and trim the main (more on this below).

HOW WEIGHT AFFECTS BALANCE

On a small boat the distribution of crew weight can change your boat's balance. Note the bow wave on the lee side of the boat in Figure 5-4. When a boat heels, the bow wave on the lee side becomes larger and tends to shove the bow to windward, and heeling puts the center of effort out over the water.

Imagine your sailboat in a flat calm with the mainsail and boom hanging way out over the water as if you were on a run. Someone comes alongside in a small powerboat and pushes the end of your boom in the direction your boat is pointing. In response, your bow turns away from the powerboat (into the imaginary wind), because the push at the end of a lever arm (your boom) has caused your boat to pivot around its keel. This in effect is what happens when you are reaching, running, or heeling: more weather helm develops because your boom and sails—and therefore your CE—are out over the water, not over the deck.

In a light breeze, a small sailboat can be steered without using the rudder by shifting crew weight from one side of the boat to the other. Lee helm results when the crew *hikes out*—sits on the high side of the boat with as much weight outboard as is comfortable and safe. This is generally done to flatten the boat and keep it from heeling excessively. To produce weather helm, ask the crew to sit to leeward. If you are steering and you don't feel the helm or the boat isn't gaining any forward momentum, you should try to sit on the low side, too.

Figure 5-4. As a boat heels, the leeward bow wave pushes the bow to windward.

HOW TO STEER WITHOUT USE OF TILLER OR RUDDER

- Close-hauled course—trim jib reasonably flat, luff main to fall off, trim main to head up
- Reaching course—ease main to reduce weather helm in order to sail straight
- Running course—heel boat to windward with main eased out in order to sail straight

Figure 5-5. In light air, create heeling by sitting to leeward.

Even in the lightest wind, a near flat calm, a light boat like a Colgate 26 will move if everyone sits to leeward and the sails gain a little shape.

Sail shape also affects a sailboat's balance. If the mainsail has a tight leech, weather helm will be increased. You will see this if the batten ends are pulled slightly inboard, to windward. To cure a tight leech, ease the mainsheet, then the boom vang, or tighten the backstay, which bends the mast.

CE can be moved in a few other subtle ways. If a mast is *raked* (tilted) aft, the sail area is moved aft. Raking a mast means leaning, not bending it. To lean it aft, ease the headstay. Another way to change the balance of the boat is to leave the center of effort in one place and move the center of lateral resistance forward or aft. Since CLR is the center of the underwater lateral plane of the boat, the only way to move it (without a centerboard) is to submerge less or more of the boat. You can push the bow down by moving crew or equipment forward, which results in increased weather helm as CLR moves forward. The opposite results if you push the stern down, allowing the bow to lift higher out of the water. As a memory aid, think of the bow being blown to leeward by wind as more of it is exposed (because you have too much weight in the stern).

A well-designed sailboat has slight weather helm, which increases as the wind velocity increases. The weather helm creates lift for the rudder and lets you feel the boat as you steer it. That feeling is a slight tug that allows you to ease pressure on the tiller and let the boat come up closer to the wind. It is hard to sail a boat with no feel because you constantly have to steer up toward the wind as well as away from the wind.

TO CORRECT TOO MUCH WEATHER HELM

- Ease mainsheet or traveler
- Reduce heeling by hiking
- Reduce mainsail area or effectiveness by carrying a slight luff, freeing the leech, or reefing
- Put up a jib (if none up) or a larger jib
- Reduce mast rake
- Move crew or equipment aft

You also want some weather helm because this allows the boat to automatically head up in puffs. Remember that apparent wind comes aft in puffs; when a boat with some weather helm naturally heads up in a puff, its heeling is reduced and the angle the wind originally made with the sails is maintained.

HOW THE KEEL AND HULL SHAPE AFFECT STABILITY

If you put a heavier keel on your boat to keep it more upright, the gain in stability might be offset by the increased weight of the boat. Although the boat might be able to stand up to more forces, the hull will sink deeper in the water, which results in greater water volume pushed aside. All this adds up to increased resistance because the weight of the boat displaces more water.

Weight in the keel is not the only thing that keeps the boat upright. The shape of your hull is also a factor. A wide, flat hull will have more stability than a narrow one. Imagine a raft that is 6 feet wide and one that is 12 feet wide. The wider raft will be able to carry more people standing on its edge without tipping over than the narrower one. As the side with all the weight sinks, the other side lifts out of the water; the wider it is, the more area there is to be lifted out of the water.

There is a difference, however, between *initial stability* and *ultimate stability*. A flat raft has high initial stability because it takes a lot of weight to tip it just a little bit. But the deeper the weighted side sinks into the water, the less additional weight is needed to sink it farther. The raft will tip over very easily after it gets to a steep angle, and it therefore has poor ultimate stability.

A deep, narrow boat with a heavy keel may tip the first few degrees very easily, but as the heel angle lifts the keel higher and higher, the more effective it becomes. So the deep keelboat may have poor initial stability but excellent ultimate stability.

HOW TO CONTROL STABILITY

Stability is essentially controlled by the relationship between the *center of gravity* (CG) and the *center of buoyancy* (CB). The boat's CG is the center of the earth's gravitational pull on that particular boat. If the boat were suspended from a wire attached to its exact center of gravity, it would remain perfectly level. The CB of the boat is the center of gravity of all the water that the hull displaces—the center of all the buoyant forces pushing up on the hull.

While CG remains in one spot because hull shape

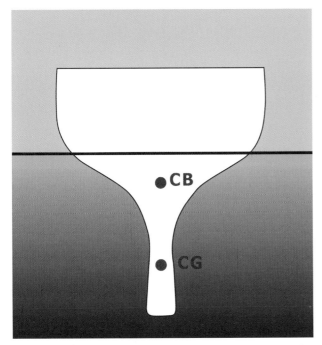

Figure 5-6. A keelboat at rest; center of gravity (CG) and center of buoyancy (CB) are in line.

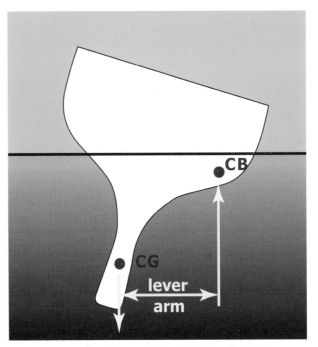

Figure 5-7. A keelboat with a slight heel; CB moves to submerged side, CG swings laterally away.

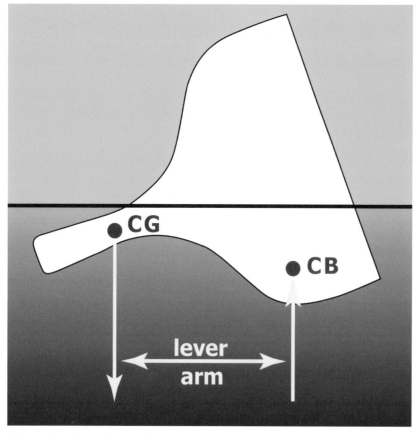

Figure 5-8. A keelboat after a knockdown; righting moment is at its greatest.

doesn't change, CB shifts to whatever part of the hull is most submerged. As the boat heels, one side submerges and the other side comes out of the water causing CB to move farther to the submerged side.

When a keelboat is at rest, sitting perfectly upright (Figure 5-6), CB and CG are in line, one above another, and CG is very low. As it heels, CB moves over to the submerged side to leeward and CG swings laterally to windward (Figure 5-7), creating a righting moment or lever arm. As the two move apart, stability produced by the lever-arm increases, with gravitational forces pulling downward at CG and buoyant forces pushing upward at CB.

Sometimes a keelboat can heel over until the spreaders are in the water and the keel and rudder are near the surface of the water (Figure 5-8). This is called a *knockdown*. Though this is a rare occurrence, you should know why it happens. The distance between CB and CG is now the greatest it has been and the righting moment is greatest too. The lever arm is longest, the sails are angled away from the wind, and the wind has lost its ability to heel the boat farther.

If you take your sails down or luff them completely, the keel's weight should eventually right the boat. But if the boat tips farther (and provided water can't get inside) the boat will go over. First it *turns turtle* (goes upside down), then continues turning until it is right side up again and the CG returns to its lowest point.

A boat that can always right itself is said to have *positive stability*. Instructors have tried to knock the Colgate 26 flat, but the boat has always come back to an upright position without turning over because it has positive stability. Even if a freak wave flipped it over, it would turn upright again.

DETERMINING SPEED

Generally, the larger the boat, the faster it can go. For a displacement boat, which is a heavy, deep-keeled boat, the maximum speed a given hull can attain from wind power is called *hull speed* and is largely dependent on the waterline length of the boat.

Hull speed is expressed as $1.34 \sqrt{LWL}$. A Colgate 26 has a waterline length of 20 feet, so it should be able to sail 1.34×4.47 or approximately 6 knots.

Figure 5-9. *Left:* Boat is traveling below hull speed (note small waves along hull).

Right: Hull speed is shown in one long wave between the bow and stern.

Figure 5-10. When sailboats surf, hull speed is exceeded.

A keelboat cannot travel faster than the wave it creates. The speed of a wave is 1.34 $\sqrt{l}$, where l is the distance between the crests. This distance increases proportionally as the height of the wave increases. So the higher the wave, the greater the distance between crests and the faster it travels.

As boat speed increases, the greater the volume of water the bow has to push aside, and the larger the bow wave becomes. As the bow wave increases in height, the distance between its crest and that of the wave following it (the quarter wave) increases until it approaches the waterline length of the boat itself. At first there are numerous small *transverse* waves while the boat travels slowly, as shown in the left panel of Figure 5-9. These spread out as the bow wave increases in height until hull speed is attained and there are only two waves along the hull—the bow wave and the quarter, as shown in the right panel. To push a heavy displacement boat past its theoretical hull speed, though possible, would take more power in wind and sails than most boats can withstand.

Many sailboats, like a Colgate 26, really don't have a hull speed. They are technically *planing* boats, able to skim along the surface of the water like a skipping stone rather than plow the water aside. A boat that planes usually has a V-shaped hull near the bow and a fairly flat bottom aft. As speed increases the bow rides up on the bow wave and finally the boat levels off at planing speed with the bow wave well aft.

Most powerboats act this way. At lower speeds the boat plows through the water. Then as the speed increases and the bow wave moves aft, the bow rises up in the air. At a certain speed the unsupported bow, with the bow wave well aft, levels off as the boat breaks into a high-speed plane. For a sailboat, its ability to plane or not depends on its length/weight ratio. If it is too heavy for its length, it will never be able to plane.

A displacement boat can exceed its theoretical hull speed by *surfing*. The boat in Figure 5-10 (see previous page) is being carried by a wave just the way surfers ride a wave on a surfboard. In large wave conditions, when running downwind, a sailboat can get on the front side of a wave and carry it for quite a number of seconds with a tremendous burst of speed. It takes practice and concentration to get on the wave just right and reap the greatest benefits and thrill. When this happens, you get a real high. Though light planing boats tend to surf more easily, displacement boats are perfectly capable of surfing—and these boats can far exceed their theoretical hull speed when they do.

SAILING DINGHIES

Although this book focuses largely on sailboats with keels, you will probably have an opportunity to sail on a dinghy. Perhaps you'll find a Laser, 420, Optimist, or Sunfish at a resort or near home. Since they capsize easily, the cardinal rule is to *stay with the boat*. You should also wear a life vest, sail with a companion or tell someone about your plans, and wear a wetsuit or warm clothing if the water is cold.

SAILING DINGHIES

To get back aboard a dinghy after a capsize:

1. Free the mainsheet.
2. Rotate the bow into the wind.
3. Put all your weight on the daggerboard or centerboard.
4. Climb in as the boat comes upright.

MORE MUST-KNOW KNOTS

The *clove hitch* is a great knot for securing fenders to lifelines or stanchions or for fastening a rope around a post, because it is held in place by friction. It is even more effective when you add a *half hitch* or two for safety. To practice this knot, find a horizontal bar, like the rung of a chair. Hold one end of the line in your left hand as if it were the line already tied to the boat. With your right hand (1) take the line over the horizontal bar and back across the fixed end (in the left hand). Then (2) go over the bar to the left of the first loop and (3) bring the end up under the left loop and pull tight.

Two half hitches

Clove hitch

How to tie a clove hitch

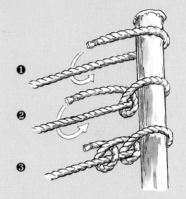

How to tie two half hitches

You use two half hitches when securing a line to a post because it is easy to tie, adjust, and untie. To practice, place the bar in a vertical position and hold one end as before, as if the line were tied to something on the boat. (1) Loop the free end around the stick and (2) go under the line and back through as if you were going to make a knot. (3) Then go around the line again in the same way. The two half hitches will hold tight against each other.

TEST YOURSELF

Balance and Stability

1. Identify which dots represent CLR and CE.
2. What is weather helm?
3. What is lee helm?
4. Does this boat have weather or lee helm?

Center of Gravity, Center of Buoyancy

To test your understanding of the relationship between center of gravity and center of buoyancy, answer the questions below.

1. When a keelboat is at rest (upright), where is the center of gravity (CG) in relation to the center of buoyancy (CB)?
2. What happens to CG and CB when a keelboat heels slightly?
3. What happens to CG and CB when a keelboat is knocked flat?

6 *HANDLING HEAVY WEATHER AND RESCUING CREW*

Many sailors describe their sailing experiences as 90 percent pure bliss—and 10 percent confrontation with the water devil. A nice day on the water can include a stop at a beautiful anchorage for lunch or a swim and end with a peaceful sunset. But you may also find yourself out on the water when an ominous storm approaches. This chapter will teach you how to reduce sail area in heavier conditions and handle emergencies like crew overboard.

SAILING IN HEAVY WEATHER

You won't always be able to control your sailing conditions. A beautiful morning could turn into a heavy squall in the afternoon, so knowing how to handle a sailboat in changing weather is important. And once you learn how to sail in heavier conditions, you will enjoy it—sailing in heavy weather is usually an adrenaline rush. If you know how to make your boat and everyone aboard comfortable, you will enjoy the exhilaration when the wind pipes up.

When you start taking lessons, what you might consider lousy weather ashore is a great learning experience for the new sailor. We know a cruising-boat owner who likes to race. Every spring he picks the windiest day he can find to go out and practice. This helps him gain complete confidence in his boat, his equipment, and his crew. He believes when everyone is comfortable in a lot of wind—both with the boat and with each other—sailing on a calmer day is a breeze.

Sailing in heavier conditions is a valuable experience. Until you've sailed in a great deal of wind or been caught

in a passing squall, you haven't tested your ability to handle the boat in a heavy wind situation. But if the prospect of sailing in heavier conditions is worrisome to you, think about the worst that can happen and then learn how to handle your boat and your crew in that situation.

Your main concern might be losing someone overboard. After you study the techniques covered later in this chapter, you should practice recoveries by throwing a cushion or floatable object overboard. Do this until your reactions become second nature. Time how fast you retrieve the object after it hits the water, bringing the boat to a complete stop when you get alongside. Practice in all kinds of weather—in a flat calm, on a moderately windy day, in a squall.

Heavy weather also puts a lot of stress on your rigging. In very severe conditions, the mast can break. Though you can't practice loss of a mast, you can be prepared for that eventuality. If your mast breaks on a small boat, you should anchor as quickly as possible and sort out all the mess without drifting farther offshore. Once you've cleaned up the failed mast and rigging, a paddle will help you get back to shore if you don't have a motor. When you start cruising on larger boats, where everything is so much bigger, there is more to consider.

When you are confident that there is nothing that can happen to you or your boat that you can't handle, then all the rest is just sound and fury. It is natural to be a bit apprehensive or frightened of big winds at first; but soon you will find that you actually enjoy the heavy stuff and look forward to that occasional confrontation with nature.

> *"I wanted confidence. My husband knows it all—and if something happens I want to know how to handle the boat. We sail weekends on Chesapeake Bay and plan to retire and go cruising within 18 months."* **CINDY SMITH (50), ANNAPOLIS, MD**

HEAVY WEATHER PREPARATION

- Check weather forecasts before you go out (visit www.weather.com or www.nws.noaa.gov).
- Take warm clothing and foul-weather gear.
- Make sure you have a lot of line, an anchor, and distress signals aboard.
- Take a way to communicate with shore—a VHF radio or a cell phone (if you are close to shore).
- Learn to read clouds while sailing.
- Be prepared to reduce sail area or change sails.
- Then, enjoy!

WHAT TO DO IN A SQUALL

When you get caught in a squall, first reduce the amount of sail area you are carrying. On a Colgate 26, you can do this by *reefing* the mainsail and furling the jib. Why should you reduce sail area? Remember, your sails are the boat's power and make the boat heel. Sail area at the top of the mast heels the boat more than sail area lower down. Reefing lowers the sail area (and the CE) and heeling is, therefore, reduced. In Figure 6-1, the boat in front has not reefed its mainsail yet; notice how the unreefed boat is sailing at a slightly greater angle of heel than the boat behind, which has reefed its mainsail. Though the wind is not overbearing, it is strong enough to give the boat behind a little more comfort and control.

As soon as you see a squall approaching, take action before it gets to you. In the end, the squall may not be that bad—sometimes a nasty looking sky turns out to be only dark clouds and rain, not more wind. If you decide not to reduce sail as the squall approaches, you should at least be prepared to do so at a moment's notice. When a bad squall hits, the wind can go from 10 knots to 40 or 50 knots in seconds.

Halyards should be neatly coiled and ready to run (see Chapter 10). Crew members should be briefed on their responsibilities; if the squall is a

Figure 6-1. The difference between a reefed mainsail (right) and a full mainsail.

bad one, everyone on board should know the procedure so not a second is lost to giving orders. This kind of preparation also has a secondary advantage: it can decrease the chance of panic. When the first blast of wind hits, the boat will probably heel over dramatically. That is when the brain process of even some experienced crew tends to go awry. Let everyone know what they are expected to do well in advance so they don't have to think.

On a small boat, the mainsail has greater sail area than the jib, so reef it before furling the jib. If you are still overpowered, furl the jib too (Figure 6-2). As the wind increases ease the mainsheet to reduce heeling. If you were sailing close-hauled before the squall hit, you will find you are steering more of a close reach in heavier winds because of the strength and weight of the wind and sea.

If you reefed your sails but you are still having difficulty maintaining control, lower all your sails and run before the wind *under bare poles* (without any sails up)—unless there is a chance of running aground. In this case, your best safety aid may be your anchor. If visibility is down to a few feet and you can't be sure of your position and are afraid you may be blown ashore, get your anchor over the side anyway. You may not have enough line to reach bottom in your current location, but you can be fairly sure that the anchor will hook before you get into water shallow enough for your boat to go aground.

Figure 6-2. Sailing with reefed main and no jib.

JIFFY REEFING

A. To reef main, lower halyard enough to hook luff cringle

B. Tighten leech line to stretch foot of sail along boom

C. When settled down, tie a safety line

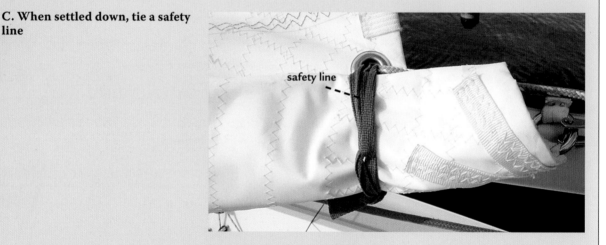

Many sailboats have jiffy reefing. Reef points and the control lines for reefing are all built into the mainsail and rigging, which makes reefing your main a quick and easy job. Below is the procedure for jiffy reefing your mainsail.

1. Ease the mainsheet and vang.
2. Lower the main halyard just enough to place the *luff cringle* on a hook at the *gooseneck*—where the boom is attached to the mast (A).
3. Winch the main halyard up tight before you do anything else (note tight luff along mast above cringle in photo above).
4. Ignore any flapping sail material for the time being.
5. Tighten the line that runs through the *leech cringle* until the foot of sail is stretched tight (B).
6. Trim the mainsheet and vang so you can start sailing comfortably.
7. When you're settled down and sailing comfortably, tie the safety line through the leech cringle and around the boom in case the reef line breaks (C).
8. Tie excess sail along the boom at the reef points as in Figure 6-2.
9. To shake out the reef, follow the above steps in reverse order closely. Make sure you untie the excess sail along the foot first, to avoid ripping the sail where you originally tied it at the reef points along the boom.

DISTRESS SIGNALS

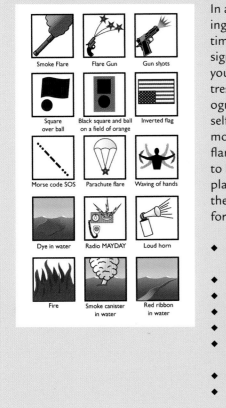

In all the years we have been sailing, we can't remember a single time when we had to use distress signals to seek help. Nevertheless, you should know how to use distress signals and be able to recognize the official signals yourself. You should also have one or more of these aboard. Some, like flares, have a shelf life and need to be checked periodically for replacement. Of these signals, only the 8 listed below are practical for small sailboats.

- Red star shells (flares or flare gun)
- Fog horn (loud horn)
- Orange and black flag
- SOS sounds
- Mayday on radio
- Code flags N and C (November and Charlie)
- Wave arms up and down
- Smoke flare

"Even though I have had my 35' sailboat for several years, sailing on Lake Michigan, the Offshore School courses improved my skills and boosted my confidence. I can now sail at night and in heavy conditions with ease and knowledge acquired during the classes. It was worth every penny."
ROBERT KOLODZIEJCZYK, MD (50), BLOOMINGTON, IL

QUICK STOP RECOVERY METHOD

- Throw a flotation device
- Shout "Crew overboard!"
- Designate a spotter
- Tack with the jib cleated and come to a stop
- When abeam of the person in the water, turn quickly to come alongside
- Toss a heaving line
- Pull the person aboard

CREW OVERBOARD!

When a person falls overboard, immediately throw them a flotation device. At the same time shout, "Crew overboard!" and designate one of your crew as the *spotter*. The spotter should keep a constant eye on the overboard crew and continually point at them.

The surest way to recover your crew in the water is to stop the boat immediately. This is called the *Quick Stop Recovery Method*. Tack the boat with the jib cleated, no matter what point of sail you are on. This will backwind the jib and slow the boat almost to a stop as in position 2 in Figure 6-3. The boat can then be maneuvered back to the person overboard to make the recovery. Without changing your sail trim, circle back to the person in the water. When you are able to turn into the wind on your last approach to come alongside that person (6), let your sails luff to come to a stop. If you are running downwind and someone falls overboard, do a quick tack and trim your sails to get back to the person in the water, as shown in Figure 6-3. If a spinnaker is set, someone should release its halyard as you tack, which causes it to fall on the foredeck and not in the water.

Every circumstance in recovering crew overboard has its own idiosyncrasies. You could be in heavy wind and steep seas, you might be in low visibility, it can happen when there's hardly any wind and the seas are flat calm. So it's very important to practice often in a variety of conditions and on different points of sail: while sailing close-hauled, on a reach, or a run.

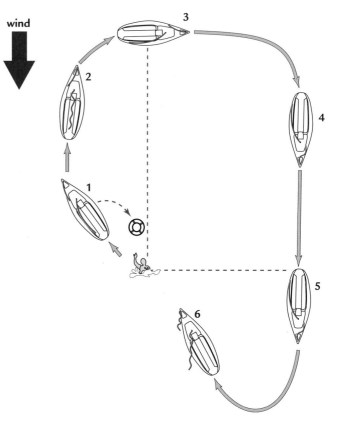

Figure 6-3. Quick Stop Recovery Method.

The *LifeSling Method* is best used on larger boats when there are only two of you aboard and one falls overboard, leaving the other crew alone. It is also a good technique in bad conditions when it is hard to maneuver alongside the person. A LifeSling is a floating lifting sling attached to the boat by a long floating line. You can buy LifeSlings in most boat supply stores. Immediately throw the sling over (3) and circle the person until they can grab the circling line and get to the sling (7). Stop the boat with the quick stop procedure outlined above, pull the person to you, attach a tackle arrangement to a halyard and the sling, and hoist the person aboard.

On small, maneuverable boats the *Mooring Pickup Method* is as fast as the Quick Stop Recovery Method and gets the boat closer to the person during the entire maneuver. Regardless, toss a floating cushion just in case. When you are close-hauled or reaching, jibe around immediately and shoot into the wind alongside the person. On a run, don't jibe! Harden up, tack, and shoot into the wind. The only difference between this and picking up a mooring is the time span. You need to do it fast!

A variation on this method is called the *Quick Turn Recovery Method*, which may be easier to use in heavy weather since it does not include a jibe. As soon as someone goes overboard, sail on a beam reach a maximum of four boat lengths, tack rather than jibe, and sail on a broad reach until you are to leeward of the person. Then turn into the wind as if picking up a

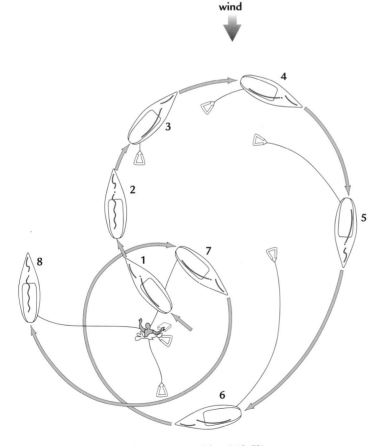

Figure 6-4. Crew overboard recovery with a LifeSling.

mooring. Stop alongside by luffing or backing the sails. Heave a line to the crew, attach him to the boat, then get him or her aboard.

These four methods of picking up a crew member who has gone overboard are all different but achieve the same goal. Which one you use depends on the wind and wave conditions, type and size of your boat, number of crew you have aboard to help you, and your lifesaving equipment. Some things common to all four procedures are: shout "crew overboard" immediately; designate a spotter; toss a lifesaving flotation device overboard; stay close; stop the boat alongside the person in the water.

TEST YOURSELF

Handling Heavy Weather and Crew Overboard Techniques
To test your knowledge of heavy weather and how to rescue someone who goes overboard, answer the questions below.

1. How should you prepare for heavy weather?
2. What should you check before you set out?
3. If a squall hits and your boat is overpowered, what should you do?
4. Name three things you do immediately if someone goes overboard.
5. Describe the Quick Stop Recovery Method.
6. What is a LifeSling?
7. When should you use the LifeSling method?

7 MOORING, DOCKING, AND ANCHORING UNDER SAIL

When your day of sailing is over, you may be dropping the anchor or picking up a mooring in a peaceful anchorage or you may end up comfortably tied to a dock in a quiet marina. This chapter will give you the knowledge to pick up a mooring, and anchor or dock under sail, without the assist of an engine.

MOORING PICKUP WITHOUT A MOTOR

Unfortunately, a sailboat without an engine doesn't have the brakes of a car or the reverse gear of a propeller to help it stop. The only way a sailboat, using only the sails, can stop is by heading into the wind. Sure, you can luff your sails and this will slow you down; but you won't come to a complete stop unless you head directly into the wind. Even if you point the boat (called *shooting* the boat) directly into the no-go zone, your boat will gradually slow down—not come to an immediate stop.

In order to stop with your bow at a mooring buoy, you must judge how far the boat will shoot. Pick an imaginary spot as your *shooting point*—the spot where you will turn toward the buoy—that is downwind of where you want to stop. The distance between this point and your stopping point will vary greatly with different wind and wave conditions, and with different hull types.

The stronger the wind, the shorter the distance you can shoot. The boat stops faster because of great resistance made by the flapping sails and rigging facing the wind, and because waves are usually higher in heavy winds. As you turn your bow into heavy wind, it tends to slam into the waves created

APPROACH A MOORING ON A REACH

- It is easy to reduce or accelerate speed
- It is easy to fall off or head up
- No tack or jibe is necessary
- In heavy winds and choppy seas, the boat stops quickly and makes the shooting point closer
- In a light breeze and flat seas the boat shoots farther and is slower to stop, making the shooting point farther downwind

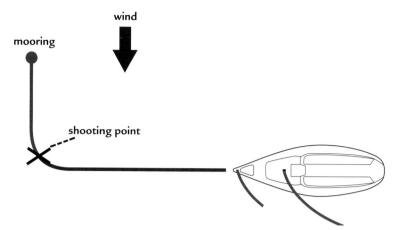

Figure 7-1. Approaching a mooring on a reach.

by the wind. In lighter air it will take longer for the boat to stop, even though it is going slower. Make sure you allow for more room in these conditions.

The approach to the shooting point that allows the most flexibility is a reach (Figure 7-1). If you approach your turning point on a close-hauled course and experience a wind shift, you may have to tack to get there. If you approach on a run, you will find it difficult to judge the turning point accurately or reduce speed easily. Also, with the mainsail set so far out for the run, you cannot slow down by easing the mainsail farther as you spin into the wind. On a reach, however, you have both speed control and directional control. You can luff or trim the sails for less or more speed, and you can head up or fall off to adjust your approach to the shooting point.

As you round up into the wind, free the sheets and let the sails luff completely. If you don't release the jib, it might back (wind will be on the leeward side), forcing the bow away from the wind and the buoy. As you travel from the shooting point to the buoy, you may want to stay at a position pointing 10° to 20° toward the desired tack with your sails luffing. That way, if you miss the buoy, you can just trim in the sails and fall off slightly to get moving again. Though you probably won't come to a complete stop, there is no chance of falling off accidentally onto the wrong tack toward other moored boats with this method.

If you find you misjudged the turning point and are approaching too fast, back the main—push the mainsail out against the wind—to slow the boat quickly. Keep your bow headed into the wind and push the boom out at right angles to the boat. If you continue to hold the boom out after the boat has stopped, the boat will start sailing backward.

Practice stopping the boat by backing the main as often as you can. To sail well is to have complete control at all times. It's important to learn how to sail the boat backward because quite often, when you leave a mooring, the boat starts drifting backward naturally. Your sails are luffing (the boat is in irons) and moving the tiller doesn't have any effect. To get underway and gain control, back the main by pushing it out against the wind and turn the rudder to fall off on the desired tack. When you are about 45° from the true wind direction, you can trim your sails and go forward.

TO SAIL BACKWARD

- Back the main
- Push the tiller toward the main
- At 45° to the true wind, trim the main, center the rudder (bring the tiller to midship), trim the jib, and the boat will go forward

HOW TO ANCHOR UNDER SAIL

Proper anchoring technique is a skill you will use in both fair and foul weather. When heavy weather hits, anchoring in a protected harbor may be your best way of avoiding the worst of the storm. When the weather is fair, a night in a serene anchorage may be part of your planned itinerary. This section covers the proper technique for anchoring under sail.

When you are ready to anchor, several decisions come into play. Look for sheltered, calm water where there isn't much wind or current. Never anchor in a channel. Check the chart to make sure there will be enough water under your keel at low tide. Then choose a spot with enough room to swing without hitting other anchored boats, obstructions such as submerged rocks and shallow areas, or swinging too close to shore.

Your anchor is either kept in an anchor locker on the bow or stored in a lazarette in the cockpit. Bring it out on the foredeck, coil the anchor line so it will run free, and secure the *bitter end*—the end of the anchor line not attached to the anchor—to a cleat on the boat.

You may think this is a silly, unneeded directive, but many anchors are lost because someone forgot to tie it to the boat.

Since you will be sailing right up to the point where you want to anchor, your halyards should be ready to drop and crew members should know they will need to ease the main and the jib as soon as you head into the wind. It is actually preferable to roll up the jib completely or (if you don't have roller furling) lower and clear it off the foredeck so you have a clear area to work with the anchor.

Look around and decide where you want the bow of the boat to be when you are finally anchored. Check the depth of the water in the vicinity of that spot to determine how much *anchor rode*—the line attached to the anchor—you should use. You may eventually let out enough rode to equal seven times that depth of water. The ratio of anchor line length used to the depth of water where you are anchoring is called *scope* (Figure 7-2).

Head into the wind when you reach the spot where you want to anchor and allow the boat to coast to a complete stop before the anchor is lowered. It is always good practice to lower the anchor over the side, as

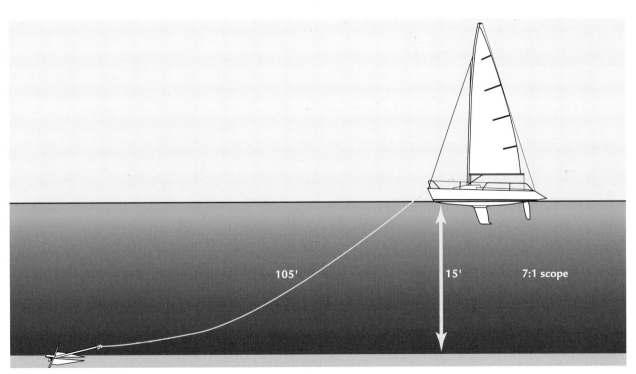

105'   15'   7:1 scope

Figure 7-2. The ratio of anchor line to depth is called *scope*.

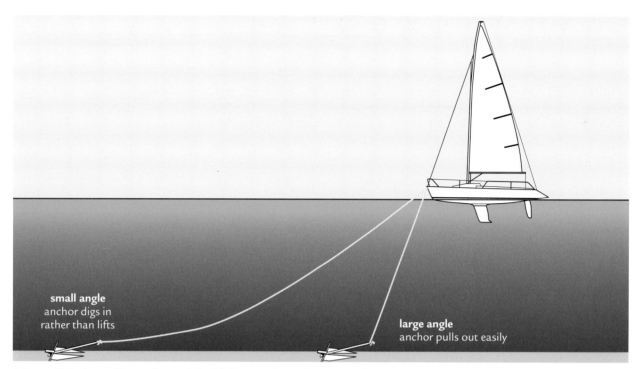

small angle
anchor digs in
rather than lifts

large angle
anchor pulls out easily

Figure 7-3. A smaller rode angle holds better than a larger angle.

HOW TO ANCHOR

- Make sure end of anchor rode is tied to a cleat on boat
- Head into the wind to stop the boat and allow the sails to luff
- Roll up or lower the jib
- When you are stopped, lower the anchor over the bow and let the boat drift backward
- Cleat the rode after sufficient scope is let out
- Check for dragging
- Lower or roll up your sails
- If you are too close to an anchored boat, raise your sails and move

opposed to throwing it overboard. Anchors have flukes that allow them to dig into the ground below; if the anchor line is tangled around these flukes, the anchor may not hold. Make sure the flukes are clear and the line can run freely.

When you head into the wind, release the mainsheet and the jibsheets. As the boat starts to drift backward, feed out your rode until you have let out five times as much line as the depth of the water. When you do this, your *scope* will be 5:1. For example, if the water is 20 feet deep, you should let out about 100 feet of line at first. In many cases, a scope of 5:1 is adequate for small boats when the bottom is good for holding, there isn't much wind, or you are anchoring for a short time. For peace of mind, increase your scope to 7:1 in a lot of wind and anytime you want to ensure you won't start *dragging*, or drifting backward.

As you let out more rode, the angle the rode makes with the bottom gets smaller; this in turn gives your anchor greater holding power (Figure 7-3). A smaller angle allows the line to pull the anchor against the bottom, which causes the flukes to dig in. With a larger angle, the rode will lift the anchor up, which can release the flukes.

Anchor lines and docklines are usually made of nylon because this type of line stretches and absorbs shock. A boat at anchor is constantly moving as current and wind direction change, however small those movements are. A speedboat rushing by can cause a wake; this is bad etiquette, but it also makes your boat bounce up and down. As the wake causes your bow to rise and fall, the anchor line needs to be able to stretch and go slack without breaking or dislodging the anchor.

When you feel you have eased out sufficient scope, snub the anchor line around a cleat. The momentum of the boat will jerk the anchor *home* (make it dig in), just as a fisherman sets the hook when a fish is caught. To check that your boat is secure and not dragging, place your hand on the anchor line forward of the bow. If you feel vibration, this usually means the anchor is dragging along the bottom.

Unless there is a lot of current or no wind at all, your boat will line up into the wind when the anchor is set. If you haven't done this already, roll up or lower your jib, then lower your main as soon as possible to avoid wear and tear on the sails.

Small sailboats, because they are so light and often have short keels or just centerboards, tend to move around more than cruising boats when anchored. From time to time, glance at points on shore and the other boats around you to see if the angle and distance have dramatically changed, bearing in mind that you may just be swinging. If you find you are uncomfortably close to another boat that was there before you, heed this rule: the boat that anchors last, moves first!

When you are ready to leave, reverse the process. Raise your main, but don't trim it in. Ask a crew member on the bow to *overhaul* the anchor line—pull it onto the boat. As he or she does this, the boat moves toward the anchor; when your bow is directly above the anchor, it usually comes up quite easily. If it seems to be stuck, take the anchor line back to a jib winch and crank it up. You may find a lot of mud or grass on the anchor as it emerges from the water. Before you bring it aboard, bounce it up and down in the water to dislodge the gunk, to avoid bringing mud aboard. When you are free and the anchor is aboard and stowed, unroll your jib, trim your main, and get underway.

If your boat has a motor, you can power toward the anchor as a crew member brings the line aboard. If you encounter resistance while you are under power, you can use the motor to move around and pull the rode from different directions until it releases. When you start sailing on cruising boats, you will learn about electric winches called *windlasses*, which help you bring up anchors on larger boats. Regardless of the size of your boat, the winches you use to help raise and trim your sails work pretty well on a stubborn anchor.

HOW TO DOCK UNDER SAIL

Docking under sail takes practice, but the techniques are easy to learn. If you take time to prepare before approaching the dock and think through each step, you will be the envy of all those type A people watching from ashore! We do a lot of women-only programs, some of which are held at pop-

"Successful docking maneuvers are the result of a combination of lots of practice, the right feeling for the size of the boat, the right timing, and an understanding of wind conditions and their effect on the docking procedure. One has to feel *how the boat is affected by the wind and* feel *how the actions taken against this take effect. Then the theory comes a lot easier."*
CLAUDIA LOGOTHETIS (35), DREIEICH, GERMANY

Figure 7-4A. On initial approach to dock under sail.

Figure 7-4B. Turned into the wind with the mainsheet eased.

Figure 7-4C. Turning alongside. Back mainsail if necessary to kill speed.

Figure 7-4D. Drifting along dock.

Figure 7-4E. Holding shroud and about to tie up.

ular boat shows. It always amazes the onlookers when five or six Colgate 26s slide into their slips or alongside a dock without a voice raised or a snag in the procedures.

In Figure 7-4, Offshore instructor Beite Cook is approaching the dock single-handed (alone). To kill speed, Beite has rolled up his jib and his mainsail is luffing (A). He has brought the boat into the wind (B). He has released the mainsheet and he's using just the boat's momentum to slip in alongside the dock (C). If he were coming in too fast he would back the mainsail against the wind to reduce speed. The boat is drifting along the dock, close enough for him to step off while holding onto the shrouds (D). Beite is ready to secure the boat to the docklines he left in place when he departed (E). He also left fenders along the dock so he didn't have to rig any on the

DOCKING PREPARATION

- Take your time and plan your approach
- Check the wind and the current
- Get docklines and fenders out
- Attach lines and fenders to the side of the boat that will be along the dock
- Have someone ready to fend off with a spare fender (particularly on larger boats)
- Roll up the jib first and sail under the main
- Make sure the main halyard is ready to lower easily
- Lower the main when you can drift into a slip or alongside a dock without sails
- If you misjudged, scull (move tiller rapidly back and forth) to get there

Figure 7-5. Tie fenders to the boat before docking.

boat; however, you should always consider placing fenders alongside the boat's hull just in case.

Well in advance of your approach, get your fenders and docklines out. Attach the docklines to cleats in the bow and stern on the same side—starboard or port—when you know which side will be alongside the dock. As shown in Figure 7-5, tie fenders to that side of the boat using a clove hitch and two half hitches, as described at the end of Chapter 5.

Gauge your approach and roll up your jib first, then sail into the marina under mainsail alone. When you feel you can drift alongside or into the dock bow-first with boat momentum only, lower your mainsail and steer without any sails. If you misjudged and can't quite make it, scull with your tiller—move it back and forth rapidly—to gain forward momentum.

In very light air you can sail into the dock with your main up as Beite did. The main can act as a brake and you can push the boom out against the wind to slow down if necessary. In heavy air, the boat will have a lot of forward momentum after the sails come down. Timing is everything. But with practice you will get to know how fast and far your boat will move as you approach with full sail, with just your main, and with no sails up at all.

Consider the safety of your crew and boat when you plan to dock. Warn your crew against using their feet or hands to fend off another boat or the dock. Don't ask a crew member to jump off the boat onto the dock until you are close enough for someone to step easily ashore. Quite often, someone is waiting on the dock to take your line, help bring the boat in close, and tie your dockline around a cleat or post for you. When you are ready to go ashore, pass your belongings to someone on the dock if you can—rather than carry them and run the risk of dropping a wallet, a phone, or your sunglasses overboard. Always check the way your boat is tied up to make sure the knots can be easily untied (but won't come undone on their own).

Wind Direction and Your Approach

Under sail, docking isn't much different from picking up a mooring or someone in the water. The boat has to be headed into the wind to stop. Although it may be blowing hard outside the marina, a relative calm usually exists when you get inside the breakwater and near the docks. The wind inside may still be strong, however. But over time you will get used to how your boat drifts in different wind strengths, so this will be less of a factor when docking under sail. Figure 7-6 shows how to approach in various wind directions: with the wind parallel to the dock (A); blowing from the dock to the water (B); and perpendicular to the dock (C).

If the wind direction is *parallel* to the dock (A), just shoot the boat into the wind and come to a stop parallel to and alongside the dock.

If the wind is blowing away from the dock and toward the water (B), shooting into the wind takes you straight into the dock, so approaching at an angle is better than head-on. If you are going too fast, remember that you can back your main to slow down. In scenario B, avoid coming in perfectly parallel to the dock. As you luff your sails to slow down, the wind will push the boat away from the dock. If the dock is long, you might be able to salvage your landing by throwing a line to someone ashore or asking a crew member to step carefully to the dock with a line before the boat slows down too much.

If the wind is blowing perpendicular to the dock and toward it from the water (C), docking is more difficult. If the wind is heavy, the best approach is without

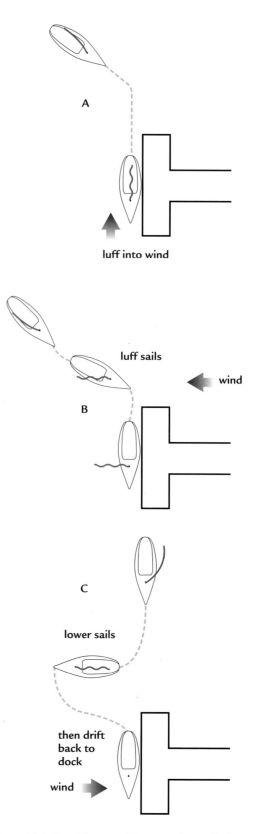

Figure 7-6. Docking a sailboat under sail alone.

any sail up. If the wind is light, you might approach with only the jib up. Round up (point your bow) into the wind to windward of the dock and lower any sails that are still up. Then drift in. If you are on a boat like the Colgate 26, you should have enough momentum to keep sailing for a short while after the sails are lowered.

Tying and Tidying Up

When tying your boat to the dock, the bow and stern lines are only half the story. If you leave the boat with just those two lines attached, any movement could cause the boat to hit the dock. If the boat moves forward, the stern swings into the dock. If it moves aft, the bow hits the dock.

To solve this problem, *spring lines* are used (Figure 7-7). The *after spring line* runs from the bow of the boat aft to a cleat or piling on the dock and keeps the boat from moving forward. The *forward spring line* runs forward to the dock from the stern and keeps the boat from moving aft. All four lines—the bow, stern, and two spring lines—keep the boat parallel to the dock.

When approaching the dock, you tied fenders along the side of your boat that would rest next to the dock. You may have had one crew member with a free fender, ready to place it between the boat and dock if it looked like the two might hit. Now check those tied fenders to make sure they will stay in place where the hull touches the dock. Ideally, the place where the dock touches the fender should be just about at the fender's middle.

Most sailboat hulls are curved. If fenders are tied too high they can pop out of the space between the boat and dock. If placed too low, where the boat curves in toward the water, they can be ineffective. Depending on the length of the fender's line, you can tie it to the lifeline or base of a stanchion. Check all your knots. It's not uncommon to see a fender floating free in a marina because a knot came undone.

DOCKING TIPS

- ◆ Spring lines keep the boat parallel to the dock
- ◆ Adjust lines from the boat, not from the dock
- ◆ Fenders should be at the proper height
- ◆ If the dock is not floating, allow for tidal changes

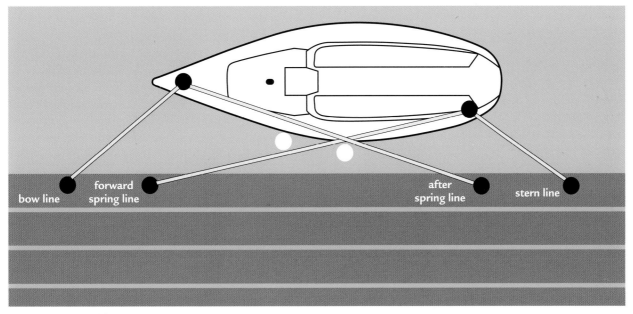

Figure 7-7. Docklines.

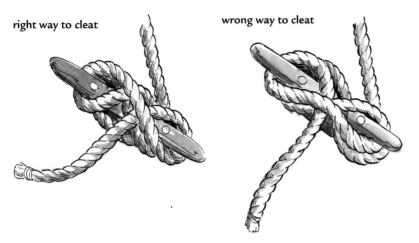

right way to cleat **wrong way to cleat**

Figure 7-8. The right and wrong way to cleat a dockline.

If you are tied to a floating dock, you don't have to worry about tidal changes. But if the dock is fixed and you arrived at high or mid-tide, make sure you leave enough slack in the lines to keep the cleats on the boat from pulling out or enough slack to keep the docklines from breaking when the tide goes out. It doesn't matter if this means the boat is sitting several feet away from the dock. You can always pull the lines in to get aboard.

Adjust your lines from the boat, not from the dock; this way, any excess line stays aboard. If someone helped catch your docklines and cleated them for you, check how those lines are tied. Sailors are a helpful group, but not all sailors know how to properly tie a bowline, a cleat hitch, or other knots used for docking.

IF YOU GO AGROUND

It's not hard for a small sailboat like a Colgate 26 to go aground when sailing in channels that constantly need dredging. Tack a little too close to the edge of the channel, and you may bump. If you keep sailing in that direction, you can truly go *hard aground* (get stuck on the bottom). So what do you do if this happens? First, think! You want to get into deeper water as quickly as possible, which is usually the direction you just came from. The stronger the wind, the more urgent it becomes to get into deep water. Greater seas (waves) come with more wind, causing your boat to pound on the shoals. If you are in a rocky area, this can result in damage to your hull if the pounding continues. Depending on the wind direction, you may also find your boat being pushed farther and farther onto the rocks.

Sometimes you can get off a sandy shelf simply by trimming the sails in tight and getting all the crew to sit or stand on the leeward side of the boat. This heels the boat and gets the keel out of the sand. Keep the boat heeled over as it starts to move forward and have someone steer toward deep water before you let the boat go upright again.

If heeling the boat doesn't work, you can try shoving the bottom with a paddle; but most likely, you'll have to *kedge off*. To do this, drop an anchor attached to the bow out in deeper water. (You might be able to throw the anchor out or get someone in a passing boat to help you.) Once you've set the anchor and you pull the line, the boat should pivot around toward the deeper water and eventually set the boat free. Don't try to kedge off from your stern or you may damage your rudder. If nothing works, wait until the tide rises. Then you can simply drift off.

TEST YOURSELF

Mooring Pickup

To test your knowledge of how to pick up a mooring answer the questions below.

1. What is the shooting point?
2. Describe the best approach to the shooting point.
3. In a strong wind, is the shooting point closer to or farther from the mooring?
4. Does the boat stop faster in heavy or light winds?

Anchoring

The questions below will test your knowledge of anchoring techniques.

1. What factors affect where you can anchor?
2. How do you prepare your crew and boat to anchor?
3. When and how do you lower the anchor into the water?
4. How do you know if your boat is dragging?
5. What is scope, and how much should you have?
6. If you go aground, how do you get off?

Docking Under Sail

Test your docking technique by answering the questions below.

1. How do you prepare for docking?
2. What do spring lines do?
3. Where should fenders be placed?
4. Which knot is best for securing fenders?
5. Why should you adjust lines from the boat?

8 RIGHT-OF-WAY RULES AND NAVIGATION

"We absolutely loved every minute! We had sailed a little before, but this gave us the confidence and knowledge to go on our own."

SUSAN WELLINGTON (50), FLOWOOD, MS

Out on the water, there are no stop and yield signs. You need to know the *Navigation Rules* (officially called the COLREGs—International Regulations for Preventing Collisions at Sea) to avoid collisions or uncertainty when in the vicinity of other boats—and that pertains to all kinds of boats, not just sailboats, in inland and international waters.

Navigating along coasts and waterways is very different from driving. There may be no road signs or lines in the water to delineate where you can sail. But there are buoys and channel markers, sounds, lights, and a *chart* (map) to guide you away from hazards.

This chapter will teach you how to sail confidently in the vicinity of other boats, and then give you an overview of the basics of navigation. There are many fine books that delve deeply into navigation—by line of sight, by the stars, and by GPS (Global Positioning System). In this chapter you will learn how to read a chart, find out where you are, avoid hazards, plot a course, and measure distance.

HOW TO DETERMINE IF YOU ARE ON A COLLISION COURSE

Before you go sailing for the first time, be aware that it is the responsibility of the person steering the boat to avoid a collision. You must be constantly on the lookout for potential trouble. If your boat is heeling and the sails block your view to leeward, peek under the boom occasionally. You might also delegate one crew member to help keep an eye out, but remember that the ultimate responsibility is yours. No excuses! Even if you know you have the right-of-way, the other boat may not be well versed on the rules, or they may not react quickly enough to avoid trouble.

If another boat is heading your way, there is one sure way of determining whether or not the two of you are on a collision course. Take a *bearing*—the angle from a point on your boat to another boat or object (Figure 8-1). Sight across your compass and note the bearing of the other boat. You can also line up the other boat with a vertical point on your boat, such as a stanchion or shroud. If, in a short time, you take the bearing again in the same way and it hasn't changed, you are on a collision course.

Another way to judge whether you are on a collision course is to watch land in the distance behind the other boat. If land is disappearing behind the bow of that boat, that boat is *making land* on your boat and will cross ahead. If land is appearing in front of its bow, as if it were going backward against the land behind it, you are making land on the other boat and will cross ahead of it. If the land remains stationary, watch out! You are on a collision course.

Relative speeds of the two boats make no difference at all. You could be sailing at 5 knots and be on a collision course with a ship traveling at 25 knots. Always be aware of your surroundings, use your eyes and your binoculars, and be ready to react when in the vicinity of other boats, rocks and shallow waters, landmarks, and buoys.

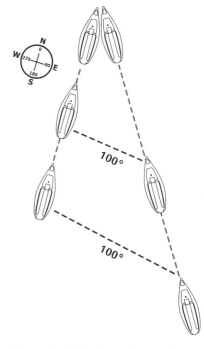

Figure 8-1. Take bearings to determine if you are on a collision course.

RULES OF THE ROAD

When Sailboat Meets Sailboat

There are only three basic possibilities, and three basic rules to follow, when your sailboat approaches another sailboat.

> Rule 1: When you are on the same tack as the other boat, the leeward boat has the right-of-way.
>
> Rule 2: When you are on opposite tacks, the starboard tack boat has the right-of-way.
>
> Rule 3: If you are overtaking the other boat, or it is overtaking you, the boat ahead (the overtaken boat) has the right-of-way.

In Figure 8-2, two boats are approaching each other and subject to the *same tack rule*. Sailors refer to the boat with right-of-way as the *stand-on vessel*—the boat that must *hold its course*. The leeward boat has right-of-way, and the windward boat has to keep clear, or *give way*. Which boat is the leeward boat? If you said the boat on the left, you were correct.

Figure 8-3 shows the *opposite tack rule*. The starboard tack boat is the stand-on vessel and has right-of-way. The port tack boat has to keep clear or give way. Which boat is on port tack? If you said the boat on the right, you are correct.

Figure 8-4 shows two boats involved in the *overtaking rule*. In this case the boat ahead is the stand-on vessel and has right-of-way. The overtaking boat has to keep clear or give way. Which boat is overtaking and what tack is that boat on? If you said the boat behind is overtaking and is on starboard

AVOID COLLISIONS

- Sight along the compass
- Line up the other boat with a stanchion or shroud
- Check if you're making land, staying the same, or losing land on the horizon
- If the angle or object on shore stays the same behind the other boat, you are on a collision course
- Difference in speed is not a factor

SAME TACK RULE

- Leeward boat is the stand-on vessel
- Leeward boat has the right-of-way
- Windward boat has to keep clear (give way)

OPPOSITE TACK RULE

- Starboard tack boat is the stand-on vessel
- Starboard tack boat has right-of-way
- Port tack boat has to keep clear (give way)

Figure 8-2. Same tack rule: boats are converging, leeward boat has right-of-way.

Figure 8-3. Opposite tack rule: boats converging, starboard tack boat has right-of-way.

Figure 8-4. Overtaking rule: boat behind is overtaking and has to give way.

OVERTAKING RULE

♦ Boat ahead is the stand-on vessel
♦ Boat ahead has right-of-way
♦ Overtaking boat has to keep clear (give way)

tack, you are correct. Note that these boats are sailing downwind, with the wind pushing from behind, and they are on opposite tacks. In the *overtaking rule*, the difference in tacks is not relevant, unless you are racing. Over many years, a complete set of rules specifically for sailboat racing has been developed and administered by the International Sailing Federation (ISAF), but these are not relevant to recreational sailing.

When Two Boats Meet, Both Using Engines

New sailors often think a sailboat always has right-of-way over powerboats, even when the sailboat is running an engine or an outboard motor. This is not so. If a sailboat has an engine or outboard motor, it is classified as a powerboat

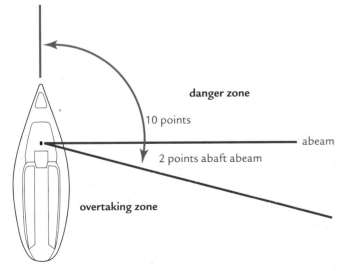

Figure 8-5. Powerboat rules: any boat in danger zone is the stand-on vessel.

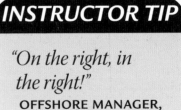

INSTRUCTOR TIP

"On the right, in the right!"
OFFSHORE MANAGER, CAPTIVA ISLAND, FL

WHO HAS THE RIGHT-OF-WAY?

- Stand-on vessel—has right-of-way, maintains course and speed
- Give-way vessel—does not have right-of-way, must alter course to avoid collision

when the engine is in use. Even if you have a daysailer with a tiny outboard motor, when the motor is running—whether your sails are up or not—you must abide by the *Navigation Rules* that apply specifically to motorboats.

Though there are many variables, the main thing to remember when boats under engine power are on a converging collision course is that the one in the other's *danger zone* has the right-of-way. The danger zone of a vessel under power is from dead ahead to two points (22.5°) abaft the starboard beam. Any boat approaching from that area is the *stand-on vessel* and has right-of-way. You are the *give-way vessel* and must keep clear.

The danger zone is described in points. That's why red and green side lights on boats are 10-point lights. A point is 11.25° and there are 32 points in a 360° circle, like a compass. Ten-point lights have a 112.5° arc, which enables you to see a red port-side light at night when a boat is approaching your danger zone.

If you are the stand-on vessel you are obliged to hold your course and speed so you won't be misleading in your attempts to keep clear. What must be avoided at all costs is the kind of mix-up that occasionally happens to pedestrians going in opposite directions on a city street. You step to the left just as the person approaching steps to the right, so you both change direction and block each other again.

On a boat, this could bring about a serious collision. If your boat is the stand-on vessel you must maintain your course. But if, in the end, the other boat has not responded appropriately and it is obvious you will collide because of that, the rules (and common sense) say that you must do whatever is necessary to avoid a collision. If two boats are approaching each other from dead ahead, both should turn to starboard. If one is approaching the other from any point behind the danger zone, it is the overtaking boat and must keep clear of the boat ahead.

When Pure Sail Meets Power

The information above should be enough to keep you out of trouble when you are running your engine and meet another powerboat. But another set of rules applies when you are sailing and meet a powerboat.

You may assume a sailboat without an engine, or a sailboat not using its engine, always has right-of-way over a powerboat. Though this is usually true, there are a few exceptions: when the motorboat is anchored or disabled; when the motorboat is being overtaken by the sailboat; and when the motorboat is a commercial vessel over 65 feet long with limited maneuverability in a narrow channel. If you see a vessel with a round black shape hoisted near the bow, it is anchored. One last point to remember: a rowboat or paddleboat has right of way over a sailboat!

NAVIGATION BASICS

How to Use a Compass

Your chief navigational aid—the compass—has certain idiosyncrasies you must understand to use it correctly. First, the compass does not point to the North Pole—*true north*—but to a magnetic mass called *magnetic north*. The

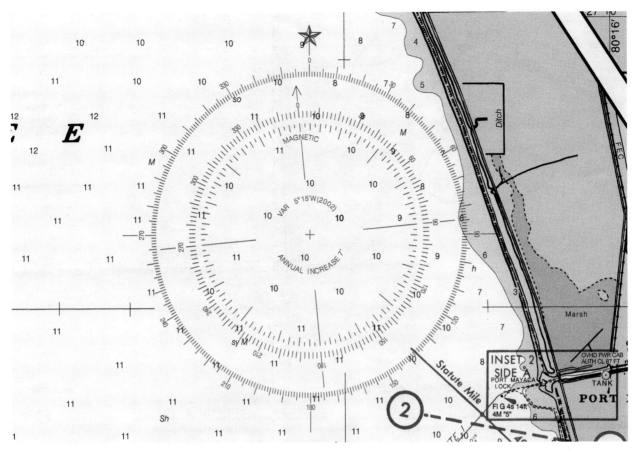

Figure 8-6. Compass rose showing two rings: outside shows true north, inside shows magnetic north.

difference between magnetic and true north is called *variation*. Variation changes with geographic location and is precalculated on the *compass roses* found on most charts.

The compass rose on a chart has two rings. North on the outer ring is true, while north on the inner ring is magnetic, which takes into account variation for the area you are sailing in. As long as you use the inner rose for plotting courses, you can forget about having to compute variation. Since your compass is magnetic, magnetic directions are all you care about, and these can be taken right off the chart.

However, compass readings can also be affected by metallic objects or electrical wiring on the boat. The resultant *deviation* usually requires that the compass be checked and adjusted when the boat or the compass is new. Although it's always there, deviation rarely amounts to more than one degree on a sailboat—and since you can't steer anywhere near that close, it is not often worth worrying about. Just be aware that deviation exists.

Accuracy is a habit you should foster when navigat-

ing. You never know when you will be caught in a dense fog and need all the precision you can muster. You should be navigating all the time, even if you know where you are.

How to Calculate Distance

Vertical lines on a chart are called *meridians* or *lines of longitude*. On a globe, meridians converge at the North and South Poles, but they show as vertical, parallel lines when the features of a round globe are projected onto a two-dimensional coastal chart for navigation. This Mercator projection method causes some distortion, but it isn't significant except at very high latitudes.

Horizontal lines are called *parallels* or *degrees of latitude*. There are 60 minutes in a degree of latitude. Each minute of latitude (and longitude at the equator) equals 1 nautical mile.

To measure distance, use the latitude gradations along the sides of the chart. Each mile is divided into tenths for accuracy and ease in measuring distance. If

Figure 8-7. Finding distance using dividers.

you want to know how far it is between two buoys, place one point of a set of dividers on one buoy and spread them so that the other point is on the other buoy (Figure 8-7). Then move them to the edge of the chart (Figure 8-8) and read how many minutes fall within the points. If the distance is 7 minutes, that converts to 7 nautical miles.

If the distance you want to measure is greater than the spread of your dividers, choose a workable distance on the chart's edge and measure that distance in minutes of latitude. A good distance is 5 miles from tip to tip. Then point one tip on your starting point, with the other resting on a spot 5 miles down the course. Rotate the points of the dividers 180°—first one tip, then the other, as you *walk* the dividers toward your destination. Normally, the last measurement is something less than 5 miles, so you will have to bring the outer tip in until it rests on your destination. Then measure this last bit of distance on the edge of the chart and add it to the number of steps you had to make. Each 180° rotation is a *step*, in this case 5 miles.

On many charts, where only a rough estimation of distance is needed, you can use your hand. The spread between your thumb and little finger might be around 10 miles, allowing you to measure 70- to 80-mile distances quickly and within a few miles of accuracy.

Many boats have speedometers, called *knotmeters*, which tell you how fast your boat is going. A knot is 1 nautical mile in an hour. Boat speed is expressed in knots, not knots per hour.

How to Plot a Course

The line between your departure point and destination is called a *course line*. When you draw a course line on a chart, you want to know the magnetic direction of the line because it represents your boat moving on a compass course. The inner circle of the compass rose on the chart equates to your boat's compass, oriented to magnetic north. It would be great if you could

Figure 8-8. Measuring distance on the side of a chart.

simply move the compass rose right over your course line and read your course direction as if it were the boat's compass. But since the rose is printed on the chart, you can't do it that way. The next best thing is to move the course line to the compass rose.

To do this, use a *parallel ruler* (Figure 8-9). This nautical gadget allows you to move a line from one chart position to another while keeping that line exactly parallel to the original line so that its direction remains the same.

Lay the edge of your parallel ruler along the desired course. Press down on one leg and move the other out in the direction of the nearest compass rose. Then press that one down and move the first in parallel. Alternately press-spread, press-spread the parallel edges of the ruler until you center one

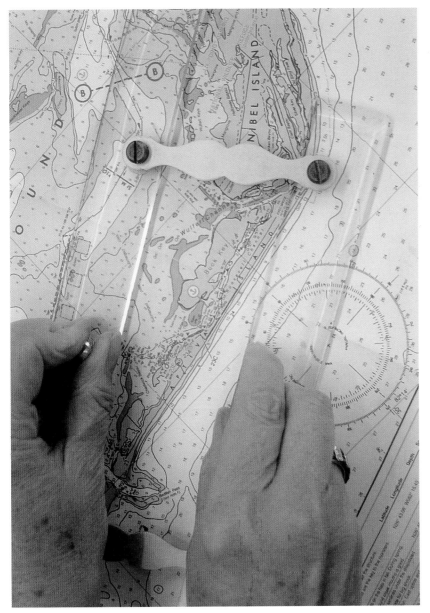

Figure 8-9. Using parallel rulers.

MEASURING DISTANCE

Bear in mind:

♦ One minute of latitude is always one nautical mile
♦ One minute of longitude is a nautical mile at the equator but shrinks to nothing at the poles
♦ So when measuring distances from chart-edge gradations, use *only* the left or right edges, *never* the top or bottom edges

TIPS FOR USING PARALLEL RULERS

♦ Press firm against the chart: if rulers slip, they are no longer parallel to your course line
♦ Read the course off the inside (magnetic) rose, not the outer (true) rose
♦ Read the correct increment: smaller rose lines are at 2°; every degree is marked on larger roses
♦ Read the correct edge of the circle for a heading—i.e., not 270° (west) when you are actually traveling 90° (east)

Figure 8-10. Typical lighted buoy.

edge directly over the cross in the center of the compass rose. Then read your course, in degrees, on the inner (magnetic) circle of the compass rose. Be sure to read the side of the compass rose pertinent to the direction you are sailing. For example, let's say you are traveling in an easterly direction somewhere between 45° and 135°. When you move your parallel ruler over the center of the compass rose, you will have two options. In this case, one side of the rose may read 104° and the other 284°. Obviously, you need to select the 104° course.

How to Read a Chart

Buoys are marked on a chart as small diamonds with a dot underneath to indicate their exact location. The color of the diamond, usually red or green, corresponds to the color of the buoy. The most common buoys are *nuns* and *cans*. Nuns are red, conical, and even numbered. Cans are green, cylindrical, and odd numbered. Next to the diamond on the chart is a notation. For example, that notation might be N "4" to indicate this buoy is a nun with the number 4 painted on it. Or it might read C "3" to indicate a can buoy marked with the number 3.

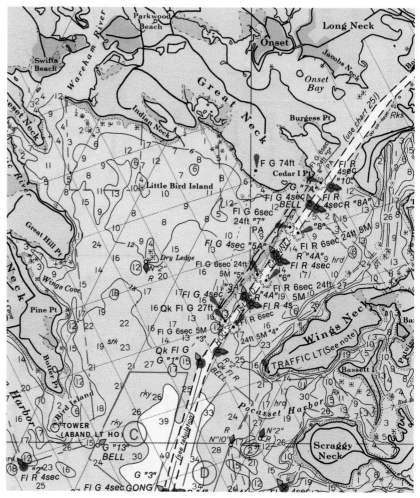

Figure 8-11. Detail of a chart.

If the dot under the diamond is in the center of a small purplish circle, it means the buoy is lighted. The characteristics of the light are written alongside. "Fl R 3 sec" means a <u>r</u>ed light <u>fl</u>ashes every <u>3</u> seconds. "FG" marks a <u>f</u>ixed <u>g</u>reen light that doesn't flash. A note on the chart like "60 FT 13 M" means that the light is <u>60 feet</u> above the surface of the water and has a visibility of <u>13 miles</u>. Study a chart and familiarize yourself with other abbreviations.

The colors on a chart are important. White areas are deep water, light blue is usually under 20 feet deep, and green is out of the water at low tide. Check how the depth is indicated. On most U.S. charts the depths are in feet at mean low water, but depths are sometimes measured in meters or fathoms. A meter is about 3 feet and a fathom is 6 feet. Also, note contour lines at certain constant depths, which give you an idea of how the bottom is laid out.

When trying to decide which side of the boat a red or green buoy should be on as you pass, remember the time-honored navigational aid for U.S. waters: *Red-Right-Returning*. This means that red buoys are kept to starboard when entering a harbor or when sailing from a larger body of water into a smaller one. If you are on the Intracoastal Waterway, the saying *Red Dirt, Green Sea* will help you remember which side to pass the markers. Red markers are on the mainland side of the channel—the dirt side—and the green markers are to seaward of the channel.

Taking Bearings

Navigation on a sailboat is slightly complicated by the fact that you can't always steer the course you want. If your destination is dead upwind, you have to tack back and forth. On a powerboat you could plot all your courses the night before and run the preset courses with only current to worry about. But when sailing, you must keep track of your location as you sail along and continuously adjust your course to the desired destination.

One of the best ways to determine your position is to take bearings. To do this, pick two or three different lights or landmarks that you can identify visually, and make sure these are marked on your chart. Sight across your compass at each one in rapid succession and record the compass heading—your bearing—to each point in degrees. A portable hand bearing compass, which you can keep in your pocket, makes it easier to take bearings as you can hold it at eye level to take readings. The first bearing you should take is the one closest to your bow or stern, since its angle changes the least.

> ### WHICH SIDE OF A BUOY SHOULD YOU PASS ON?
>
> - Red-Right-Returning—keep red buoys on boat's starboard side when returning to port or sailing from larger body of water into smaller one
> - Red Dirt, Green Sea—red markers on mainland side of channel (dirt), green markers to seaward side of channel when sailing on Intracoastal Waterway

Figure 8-12. Using a hand bearing compass.

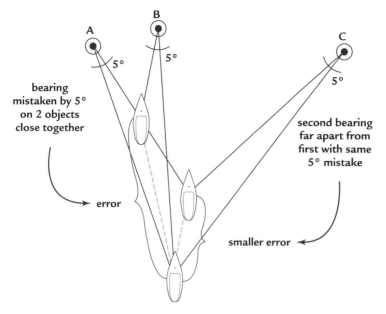

Figure 8-13. Errors in taking bearings.

Using your chart, locate the same compass bearing for each of the readings you just took on the nearest magnetic rose (inner circle). Place an outside edge of your parallel ruler on both this number on the rose and the cross in the very center of the rose. Walk the other outside edge of the ruler to the charted light or landmark you took the bearing on, then draw a line through that object and out into the water. You are located somewhere along this line. Now repeat the process using the second and third bearings you took. Three bearings will give you a small triangle—a *cocked hat*—when plotted, which is a bit more accurate than the cross you get from only two bearings. You are somewhere in the triangle. If the triangle is large, take your bearings again; one was probably inaccurate.

When you choose lights or landmarks, make sure there is a good distance between them. If you use only two bearings you will get greater accuracy if the two marks are 90° apart from your position. Figure 8-13 shows bearings taken with a 5° error in each. Note that using landmarks A and B produces a much larger aggregate error than using A and C, which are farther apart.

TEST YOURSELF

Right-of-Way Rules
Answer the questions below to test your understanding of right-of-way rules.

1. What is a bearing and when should you take it?
2. If two sailboats are on the same tack, which one is the give-way vessel and what should it do?
3. Explain the opposite tack rule.
4. Explain the overtaking rule.
5. When does a sailboat not have right-of-way over power?
6. Where is a powerboat's danger zone and when is it used?

Navigation
1. Explain variation and deviation.
2. What distance is represented by 2 minutes of latitude?
3. When using parallel rulers to plot a course, what four common mistakes should you avoid?
4. What does Red-Right-Returning mean?

9 SPINNAKER

We will conclude these lessons with a fast basic rundown of spinnaker work for those beginners, and there are always a few, who instinctively master the essentials of sailing early and thirst for the delight (and extra challenge) of sailing under this most picturesque of sails.

The spinnaker is like a large parachute that pulls the boat downwind. It can be set with the true wind direction anywhere from dead astern to about abeam. It's made of light nylon and adds so much sail area to the total sail plan of the boat that speed is markedly increased when a spinnaker is set.

The accompanying drawing shows the various lines involved with spinnaker work. The spinnaker is hoisted by the spinnaker halyard. One corner is held in place by the *spinnaker pole*, which is always set to windward, opposite the main boom. The corner attached to the pole is the tack of the spinnaker, and attached to it is the spinnaker *afterguy* or, more commonly, *guy*. The free corner of the spinnaker has a sheet attached to it like any other sail. The only tricky thing about the foregoing terminology is that during a jibe, the pole is switched over to the new windward side and the old guy becomes the new sheet (attached to the free corner of the sail) and the old sheet becomes the new guy (running through the jaws in the end of the pole).

There are two lines to hold the pole in position—the *topping lift* to keep it from falling when the spinnaker isn't full of wind, and the *foreguy* (some people call it the *spinnaker pole downhaul*) to keep the pole from *skying* (pointing way up in the air) when the spinnaker is full. (See Figure 9-1.)

PREPARATION FOR SETTING THE SPINNAKER

Starting at the head of the spinnaker, run down both edges one at a time, folding each accordion-style, holding the folds in one hand as you go. This will ensure that the spinnaker isn't twisted. If two edges are untwisted, the third one, the foot in this case, also has to be straight.

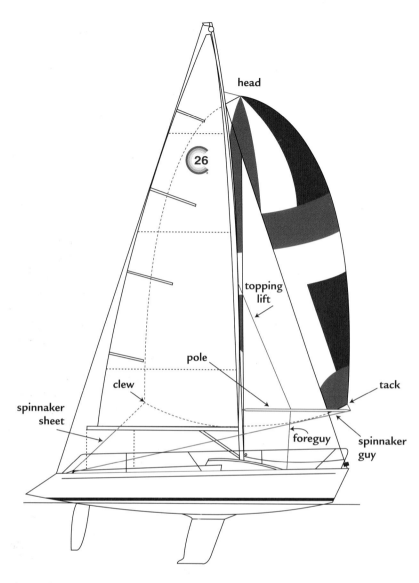

Figure 9-1. Spinnaker terminology.

Then, holding onto the folded edges and all three corners of the sail, stuff it into the container you hoist the spinnaker from. This used to be called a "turtle" because it was originally a plywood board covered with black inner tube rubber with an opening at one end. When the spinnaker was stuffed into it with the three corners hanging out the open end and placed on the foredeck of the boat near the bow, it looked like a turtle. This term has been carried over even though spinnakers are now stuffed into bags, buckets, or even cardboard boxes.

The halyard, sheet, and guy are then connected to the three corners. Make sure the halyard is attached to the head of the sail—the corner with the swivel. Since the spinnaker is vertically symmetrical, you can attach the sheet and guy to either of the other two corners. Make sure the sheet and guy are outside of everything on the boat (shrouds, stays, lifelines, or rails) before connecting them.

In the case of a Colgate 26 or larger boat, the spinnaker is usually set on the leeward side. On smaller boats, where there is danger of capsizing if a crew member goes to the leeward side of the boat, the spinnaker is set to windward and pulled around the jibstay.

Next, set up the pole to windward with the guy running through its outboard end.

THE HOIST

The key to a good hoist (set) is to separate the lower corners of the spinnaker as the halyard is being raised. Often this means cleating the sheet (which is attached to the clew) and pulling the tack of the sail out to the pole as quickly as possible with the guy, unless you have enough crew to have a person on the sheet also. The halyard should be pulled up smartly so the spinnaker will neither fall overboard nor fill with air before it's all the way up. If the latter happens, the person on the halyard may have difficulty holding on unless they get a wrap around a winch or cleat in a hurry.

THE SET

Just a few simple rules form a good foundation for basic spinnaker work:

1. Set the pole at right angles to the apparent wind. Use the masthead fly since it's in less disturbed air than the shroud telltales, and make sure the pole lies perpendicular to the masthead fly.

2. Since the spinnaker is a symmetrical sail, it should look symmetrical. Neither corner should be higher than the other. If the clew is higher than the tack, the pole should be raised to even them out.

3. The pole should be perpendicular to the mast so it will hold the tack of the spinnaker as far away from the blanketing effect of the mainsail as possible. If the pole needs to be raised, as in rule #2, don't just pull the topping lift (which raises only the outboard end), but raise the inboard end also if it's adjustable.

4. Ease the sheet until a curl appears along the luff of the "chute" (short for parachute spinnaker, as it was formerly called) and then trim it back until the curl disappears. The spinnaker trimmer will have to pay attention to the luff of the spinnaker constantly, because the moment

he or she looks away the chute will collapse almost as if it had been waiting for a moment's inattention in order to misbehave.

If you follow these few basic rules you shouldn't have any trouble learning to fly a spinnaker.

THE JIBE

There are two basic types of jibes: the *end-for-end* jibe used on small boats with a light spinnaker pole and the *dip-pole* jibe used on larger boats with a heavy pole.

We'll concern ourselves with the former, since it is applicable to the type of boat most learn on (see Figures 9-2 to 9-5). The person on the foredeck stands behind the pole facing forward. Just before the jibe the foredeck crew disconnects the pole end from the mast and from the guy at the same time. As the boat turns downwind, he or she grabs the sheet and snaps the jaw of the pole over it. Then the pole is passed across the boat and the free end attached to the mast. Meanwhile, the person in the cockpit is easing the sheet and trimming the guy as the boat turns into a jibe. This keeps the spinnaker downwind and full of air. The skipper pulls the main across and, if the wind is blowing hard, after the boom crosses the centerline, he or she turns the boat back downwind to keep it from broaching (rounding up broadside to the wind), which it has a tendency to do after a jibe.

Figure 9-2. The start of an end-for-end jibe. Detach the pole from the mast first.

Figure 9-3. Next attach the end of the pole to the old sheet. (The line that was the sheet becomes the spinnaker guy.)

Figure 9-4. Attach the pole to the mast to complete the jibe.

Figure 9-5.
Both spin-
nakers are
properly set:
tack and clew
are level.

Figure 9-6. Douse the spinnaker quickly and smartly, stowing it off the deck as quickly as possible.

THE DOUSE

Taking a spinnaker down (dousing) is much like run-ning a movie of the hoist backward. First grab the sheet as near the clew as possible and pull it into the cockpit so the spinnaker will come down behind the mainsail. Sec-ond, let the guy run free and start gathering in the foot of the sail. Third, lower the halyard fairly fast, but not so fast that you get ahead of the crew gathering it in, lest the sail fall into the water. Stow the spinnaker below and off the foredeck as quickly as possible.

10 MARLINSPIKE SEAMANSHIP

SAFE AND EFFICIENT WINCH USE

Your boat may or may not have winches, depending on its size. The larger the boat, the more likely it will need winches to overcome the larger force in the sails. The Colgate 26 has two self-tailing winches, one on either side of the boat, for the halyards, reefing lines, spinnaker guy and sheet, and jib-sheets. To *tail* a line means one person cranks on the winch while another crew member pulls the line coming off the winch to keep it taut. On a self-tailing winch the line from the drum goes over a stainless steel guide at the top of the winch and then is jammed into a cleat on the top of the drum, so a second person is not necessary. Except for the jibsheets, all the other lines lead to the winches through a *rope clutch*, as in Figure 10-1, which acts as a brake to hold a line in place when you set a sail or make other adjustments.

Figure 10-1. Here the halyard runs from the base of the mast, through a rope clutch, then to a self-tailing winch.

Figure 10-2. The proper way to put wraps around a winch.

If this is the case on your boat, close the lever of the rope clutch as you prepare to raise the halyard; then pull the halyard toward you through the clutch, hand over hand, until you can't raise the sail any further. Up to this point you should not have any of the halyard wrapped around a winch.

When you raise the sails use a winch to haul the last bit up. It is at that point that you put turns around the winch, not before. When you can't pull the sheet manually anymore, wrap one or two turns of the halyard around the winch using your fingers as you circle it as shown in Figure 10-2. Let the line slide through your fingers as you circle the winch. Do not make a loop around the winch with two hands as in Figure 10-3 or you might catch your fingers between the winch and the line. Once you have circled the winch, jam the line in the cleat around the top and crank the winch handle.

Whenever using a winch, focus on the results. If raising a sail, look aloft to be sure neither the sail nor halyard will catch behind a spreader or otherwise impede the raising of the sail. If you get unexplained resistance, look around. Make sure the mainsheet, cunningham, and boom vang are loose. When trimming a jib, look at the sail to make sure you haven't overtrimmed just as you would when easing a sheet. Always look at the sail. To ease the line, place one hand over the coils on the drum with your thumb touching

THE RIGHT WAY TO PULL ON A LINE

- Grab the line in your right hand with your fist over the top, thumb and forefinger toward you, and pull to your right side (like swimming).
- Then grab the line with your left hand, fist over the top, and pull to your left side.
- Alternate as above, until line is trimmed in (or winch is needed).
- Instead of pulling it to you, this method uses your whole arm with broader, more efficient motion.

Figure 10-3. Improper way to add wraps to a winch.

Figure 10-4. Proper way to ease a sheet on a winch.

AVOID WINCH OVERRIDES

- Start with two or three wraps and pull manually
- Add more wraps as tension occurs
- Make sure someone tails and keeps tension on the sheet
- Use one hand when adding wraps
- Add additional wraps before inserting the winch handle
- Remove the winch handle when the sail is trimmed in

your index finger as in Figure 10-4, not sticking out where it can get caught in a loop. Ease the end of the line with the other hand. Your hand on the coils acts as a brake to control speed as the line is eased. If you just uncleat the line and let it loosen on its own, the coils will first stick on the drum, then suddenly jerk out, catching you by surprise. At best, the sheet will probably go out too far and you'd have to crank it back in. At worst, your hand holding the free end could suffer rope burns or get pulled into the coils around the winch.

If you have too many wraps on a winch you may get an *override*, which occurs when the part of the line going onto the winch has crossed over and pinched the part leading off the winch. If this happens, you won't be able to continue turning the winch. Remove the turns from the winch and start again—this requires relieving the tension on the override. Using a spare line, tie a rolling hitch to the line leading to the winch that has the override, as shown in Figure 10-5. The rolling hitch won't slip under pressure, so crank it tight on another winch to relieve the original line and then untangle the override.

KEEPING LINES ORGANIZED

All lines, and particularly halyards, should be neatly coiled. When the sail is up as far as it will go, cleat the halyard, coil it, and then put the winch handle away. Never leave the handle in the winch, as it can get lost and is expensive to replace.

All the excess halyard now lying in your cockpit or on deck needs to be coiled and cleated in such a way that it can be easily uncoiled if you suddenly need to lower the main. Make your coils clockwise to minimize kinking. Always coil from the *fast end*—the end that is attached to something—toward the free end of the line to work any kinks out. How many times have you coiled up a garden hose only to find it trying to go the other way with interminable kinks? The hints in the sidebar on page 110 help you avoid that same situation with lines on a boat.

Figure 10-5. Using a spare line, tie a rolling hitch to the line that is jammed on the cleat to relieve the strain, then untangle the wraps on the winch.

KNOTS TO KNOW

A rolling hitch can slide in one direction but will stay in place when tension is applied in the opposite direction. Some common uses are: to relieve tension on another line that may have an override in it; to secure a halyard to a stanchion or rail; to tie a line to an anchor rode of a stuck anchor so you can use a cockpit winch to help bring it up; and when lashing a dinghy on deck.

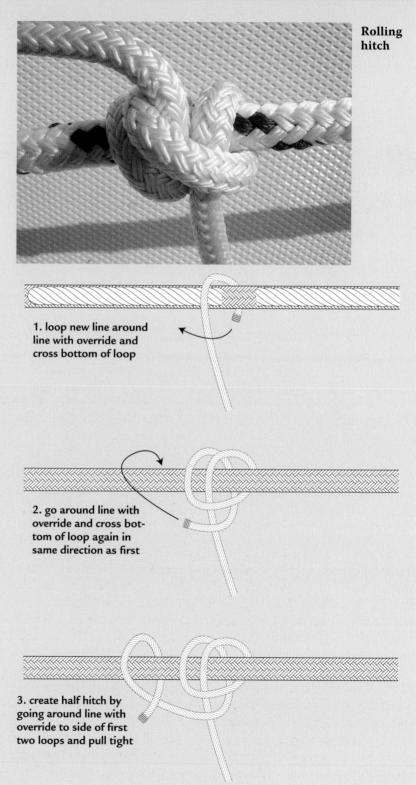

Rolling hitch

1. loop new line around line with override and cross bottom of loop

2. go around line with override and cross bottom of loop again in same direction as first

3. create half hitch by going around line with override to side of first two loops and pull tight

How to tie a rolling hitch.

TO TIDY UP A HALYARD

1. Tighten the halyard and make one turn around the base of the cleat before criss-crossing it. The last loop should be a *half hitch*, which keeps the line from uncleating accidentally.

2. Coil the line, starting from the end fastened to the cleat.
3. Reach through the coil to the cleat and pull the bottom section of the half hitch through the center and over the top of the coiled line.
4. Loop that section of the half hitch over the top of the cleat to neatly hang the halyard.

If a sudden squall hits, you need to be able to release halyards quickly, without any tangles. To do this, take the hanging coil off the cleat and flake out the halyard on the deck. The bitter end of each halyard should be secured with a stop knot so you can just let the halyard go, get on to the next emergency, and know that the halyard won't be lost up inside the mast. The jibsheets should also be coiled and laid down in the cockpit with the coils running off the top. If coils run off the bottom and you have to do a quick tack to avoid a collision, the sheet can knot up and jam in the sheet block when it is thrown off the winch.

If you didn't have time to coil and stow your docklines before getting the sails up, this should be done now. Since the docklines are no longer attached to anything, it doesn't matter which end of the line you coil first, unless there is a spliced loop in one end. If so, start with that end and bring the coils to it. It doesn't matter which hand you hold the coils in; but make your loops clockwise to avoid kinking as shown in the sidebar on page 110. Braided line has a tendency to make figure eights with each loop. That's okay; the loops don't have to be perfect ovals.

> *"A clean deck is a happy deck!"*
> **WILLIAM LEE (30), BOSTON, MA**

HOW TO COIL A DOCKLINE

1. Stretch one arm out the same distance for each coil and collect loops in your other hand.

2. Finish the coil off by wrapping the end of the line around the middle of the coils a few times, then pass a loop through the top part of the coiled line.

3. Pass the same loop over the top of the coils on either side and pull tight on the end of the line.
4. If you are hanging the line, run the bitter end through the loop (instead of passing the loop over the top of the coils), leaving enough line to hang the coil.

THREE-DAY STUDY PROGRAM

The Fast Track to Sailing program covered in this book can be completed in three days if approached in the context of a rigorous instructional setting. Spend three days learning the basics in Chapters 1 through 6. Chapters 7 through 10 touch on slightly more advanced topics—docking, rules of the road, spinnakers and lines and winches. Occasionally you should go back to the earlier chapters to refresh yourself on basic concepts. When you are finished, you will be ready to sail your own, a rented sailboat, or a friend's boat with confidence.

If you're learning on your own, outside a concentrated instructional program, proceed at your leisure, taking as long as you like to master the material in this book. Remember, learning is half the fun.

In this section, we present you with the tests that those who actually participate in Offshore Sailing School's Fast Track to Sailing® program take each day before setting out on the water. The answers to these questions are covered in this book.

Day One

1. What is LOA?
2. What is the primary purpose of standing rigging?
3. Which point of sail is 90° off the wind?
4. If you are in irons, how do you sail away on port tack?
5. If you are on starboard tack, which side is the boom on?
6. Which knot is used to make a loop in the end of a line?
7. What's the name of the line used to raise the sails?
8. What is a series of tacks to get to an upwind destination called?
9. In order to tack, do you push the tiller toward or away from the mainsail?
10. Name the three corners of a sail.
11. Name the edges between the three corners of a sail.
12. What is the difference between stays and shrouds?
13. What are topsides?
14. What is the difference between standing and running rigging?
15. What are telltales?
16. What are the commands for tacking and jibing?
17. What does hardening up mean?
18. What is by the lee?

Day Two

1. What is the fastest point of sail in light air?
2. Describe a header and a lift.
3. Describe the difference between a veering and a backing wind.
4. What is apparent wind?
5. What two functions does the keel of a sailboat perform?
6. What are some of the reasons you may be experiencing excessive weather helm?

7. What does a cunningham do?
8. What is your main concern when sailing downwind?
9. Is a full sail more or less powerful than a flat sail?
10. Is apparent wind always stronger than the true wind?
11. What happens to apparent wind in a puff?
12. If you head slowly into the wind and the top tell-tale on the jib starts to flutter on the windward side before the lower two, what does this mean and how do you correct it?
13. What should you do first if a person falls overboard?
14. What is your first maneuver when you do a Quick Stop Recovery of a crew overboard?

Day Three

1. What is the best approach when attempting a mooring shoot?
2. Does the stand-on vessel or the give-way vessel have right-of-way?
3. What scope should you use to anchor your boat overnight in normal conditions?
4. What is the same tack right-of-way rule for sailboats?
5. What is the opposite tack right-of-way rule for sailboats?
6. If a sailboat with sails up is motoring, is it a sailboat or a powerboat?
7. When should you consider reefing the mainsail?
8. What is the overtaking rule?

TIPS AND CHECKLISTS

Getting Underway

1. When you board, step in the middle of the boat—on the floorboards if the boat is a tippy one—while holding onto the shrouds, if possible.
2. If the jib is not rigged on a furling headstay—hank on the jib tack first, feeding it between your legs for control and checking along the foot for twists.
3. If jibsheets are not attached—tie them on with bowlines to the jib clew, lead them back to the cockpit winches through proper blocks, and tie stop knots in each free end.
4. If the jib halyard is not already attached—attach it to the grommet in the head of the jib; first look up and check for twists around a shroud, spreader, or another halyard.
5. If the mainsail is not flaked along the boom—feed the mainsail foot into groove on the boom; attach the tack at the gooseneck and the clew to the outhaul; pull the foot tight with the clew outhaul.
6. If battens are not in their pockets—start with the lowest one; make sure the most flexible batten is placed in the highest position; make sure all battens are pushed down into the pocket and under the flap at the leech, so they can't fly out when the sail luffs.
7. Before raising the sail—follow along the mainsail luff to remove twists; feed the luff into the groove in the mast, starting at the head; attach main halyard.

8. To raise the main—first make sure the mainsheet is completely free to run, vang and cunningham are loose, and the halyard is not fouled around shroud, a spreader, or another halyard.
9. While main is being raised—hold the boom up by hand and make sure the leech isn't caught under a spreader.
10. After the mainsail is raised and the luff is tight, cleat and coil the main halyard.
11. Raise and secure the jib, or unroll it if you have roller furling.
12. To get underway—untie the mooring line and hold onto it while backing the jib to the desired tack, then drop the mooring.
13. Don't cleat the mainsheet on a small boat in a breeze.

Sail Trim and Balance

1. When checking sail trim, adjust the jib first—ease it until it luffs, then trim in; do the same with the main.
2. Push the tiller toward the fluttering jib telltale.
3. If the leeward jib telltale flutters, steer more toward the wind or ease the jib.
4. If the windward jib telltale flutters, steer more away from the wind or trim the jib.
5. If you have a strong weather helm, reduce the heel of the boat by crew weight and/or by depowering the mainsail.

6. If you have a lee helm, place crew to leeward, bring the mainsail boom near the center of the boat with the traveler, and de-power the jib.
7. If you have high winds, you want flat sails. For light winds, use full sails.

Leaving a Dock

1. Assign jobs to your crew.
2. Double up docklines so they can be released from the boat.
3. Check the wind and current.
4. Prepare the sails and anchor for quick use.
5. Spring the bow or stern out.
6. After leaving, stow lines and fenders.

Safety Precautions When Sailing

1. Use winches properly to avoid catching fingers.
2. Don't stand to leeward of the boom or gooseneck; if either fail, they fly to leeward.
3. Don't stand or sit where you can get hit by the traveler car or tangled in the mainsheet in a flying jibe.
4. Be aware in case you suddenly run aground or hit a rock; people aboard will pitch forward.
5. Check frequently to leeward of the jib for approaching traffic and possible collisions.

6. Wear boating shoes—sailing barefoot can cause falls and stubbed or broken toes.

Tacking

1. Sight abeam to windward to estimate direction of your next tack.
2. Sight aft of abeam to windward to avoid tacking into the path of another boat.
3. Release the jibsheet when there is a large luff in the jib.
4. Watch to make sure the jibsheets don't hang up on edges of hatches or vents.
5. Turn slowly and not past 90° while the jib is being trimmed in.

Jibing

1. Give plenty of warning to the crew of your intentions.
2. Turn slightly by the lee to start the mainsail across.
3. Steer back downwind when the mainsail swings to new tack.
4. Remember not to make a large course change.

GLOSSARY

Here you'll find definitions for many of the terms we used in this book.

abeam—at right angles to the boat
accidental jibe—an unexpected boom swing. See also **jibe.**
aft—at, near, or toward the stern
aground—touching the bottom
aloft—up in the rigging
anchor—heavy object lowered in the water to keep boat from drifting
anchor rode—chain, rope, or both used to attach anchor to boat
angle of attack—angle of boat's centerline to water flow
angle of incidence—angle of sails to the apparent wind
apparent wind—the vector wind caused by the true wind in combination with the boat's forward motion; the wind you feel
aspect ratio—relation of height to width
astern—behind the boat
athwartship—across the boat
back (a sail)—to push a sail to windward (against the wind)
back an anchor—put two anchors in line attached to each other by a short length of chain
backing wind—wind direction shifting counterclockwise, such as W to SW
backstay—wire from upper part of mast aft to deck; a component of standing rigging
backwind—wind off the jib hitting the lee side of the main

balance—to neutralize forces so boat sails on a straight course with little helm
ballast—weight in keel used to increase stability
batten—a slat inserted in the leech of a sail
batten pocket—pocket for battens in the leech of a sail
beam—the widest part of the boat
beam reach—sailing with the wind abeam
bearing—the angle to an object
beat—a series of tacks
Bernoulli's Principle—as velocity of air increases air pressure decreases. Air picks up speed as it flows behind the jib and mainsail. The reduction in air pressure creates lift, causing the sails to pull the boat forward.
berths—bunks for sleeping aboard
bilge—low area of boat where liquids collect before being pumped out
bimini—awning over cockpit
bitter end—the end of a line
blanketed—deprived of wind in the sails by another boat or large object to windward
blocks—pulleys that sheets run through
boom—horizontal spar that supports foot of sail
boom vang—device to keep the boom from lifting
bow—forward end of the boat
bow line—a docking line from the bow to the shore
bowline—a common knot used by sailors

to form a loop (pronounced *bolin*)
bow wave—the initial wave created by the bow breaking the water
breast line—single line from middle of boat to opposite piling
broad reach—sailing between a beam reach and a run; sailing with the wind on the quarter
buoys—floating marks
by the lee—wind on same side of the boat as boom when running
cabin sole—floor of cabin
camber—belly of a sail
can—odd-numbered navigational buoy, usually green
capsize—to overturn a boat
catamaran—a boat with two parallel hulls
centerboard—a board or plate raised and lowered on a pivot pin to reduce leeway
centerboard trunk—housing for the centerboard
centerline—an imaginary line down the middle of the boat from bow to stern
center of buoyancy (CB)—The point around which the forces pushing upward to keep a boat afloat are concentrated. The CB will be located somewhere on the fore-and-aft centerline of a well-trimmed boat at rest, but as the boat heels and its wetted surface changes, the CB moves to leeward, thus resisting further heeling. See also **center of gravity.**
center of effort (CE)—The theoretical

point in a boat's sail plan at which the wind's pressure is focused. The fore-and-aft relationship between the CE and the center of lateral resistance (CLR) determines a boat's helm balance. See also **center of lateral resistance.**

center of gravity (CG)—The geometric center through which all weights in a boat act vertically downward. If you could suspend a boat from its CG, it would hang perfectly level. In a keelboat the CG is located deep in the hull, giving it "ballast stability." The relationship between the CG and the center of buoyancy (CB) creates a "righting arm" that causes the boat to favor an upright position. As the boat heels and the CB moves farther leeward from the CG, the righting arm grows in strength, thus resisting further heeling. (See discussion on pages 65–66.)

center of lateral resistance (CLR)—The imaginary vertical line through a boat's underwater profile that divides the underwater area into two equal halves, forward and aft. The CLR is like the axis of a weather vane. If you were strong enough to place your forefinger on a boat's CLR and push it sideways, it would yield without pivoting. The relationship between the CLR and the center of effort (CE) dictates the boat's tendency to either round up into the wind or fall off. Simply put, if the CE is located aft of the CLR, the boat will have weather helm—it will pivot toward the wind. If the CE is forward of the CLR, the boat will have lee helm. (See discussion on page 60–61.)

chart—nautical map

chock—guide on deck for docklines or anchor rode to pass through

chord—straight-line distance from luff to leech on a sail

cleat—device to secure a line

clew—the aft corner of a sail

close-hauled—sailing as close as possible to the wind

close-reach—sailing between close-hauled and a beam reach

cockpit—a recessed area in the aft deck to accommodate crew

collision course—one in which the relative bearing on another boat doesn't change and boats are converging

come about—to change tacks with the bow turning through the wind; to tack

companionway—passageway from cockpit to interior cabins below

compass—magnetic card that points to magnetic north

contour lines—lines on a chart that connect all areas of equal depth and height

cotter pin—a split pin separated and bent when inserted to keep clevis pins and turnbuckles from backing out

cringle—a reinforced hole sewn or pressed into a sail through which a line can be passed

cubbies—lockers used to store food and personal effects

cunningham—device to tension the luff of a mainsail

current—water flowing in a definite direction

Dacron—synthetic material used in sail manufacture

daggerboard—centerboard that retracts vertically rather than pivots

danger zone—on a motorboat, the area from dead ahead to two points aft of starboard beam; another motorboat converging from this direction has right of way

daysailer—small sailboat

depth sounder—electronic instrument that reads depth of water

deviation—compass error caused by metal aboard the boat

dinghy—a small rowboat used to get to shore from mooring. Can also be stepped for sailing.

displacement—total weight of the boat

dividers—two metal legs hinged at top for measuring chart distance

dock—a landing pier, wharf, or float

dog—the act of fastening down hatches

dogs—wing nuts that fasten hatches when closed

douse—quickly lowering sails

downwind—sailing with the wind pushing from behind

draft—distance from waterline to boat's lowest part

draft (of a sail)—as seen from above, the distance from the straight-line chord between a sail's luff and leech to the deepest point of the sail's curve, or camber

ease—to let out, as in a sheet

fairlead—a fitting through which a line passes, changing the line's direction

fall off—to turn the boat away from the wind

feathering—to sail so close to the wind that sails luff periodically

fin—a type of keel

flake—preparing or coiling a rope or a sail such that it will pay out without tangling

foot (of sail)—bottom edge of a sail

footing—increasing speed by falling off slightly

foredeck—the deck forward of the mast or foremast

forestay—any wire that runs from foredeck up to mast for setting a jib and supporting the mast

forward—toward the bow

fouled—tangled

fractional rig—forestay runs from bow to at least three-quarters up the mast, but not to the top

freeboard—distance from deck to the water

furl—to fold a lowered sail and secure it

galley—cooking area (kitchen) in a cruising boat

gennaker—asymmetrical, lightweight reaching jib

genoa—jib whose clew overlaps the mast

gimbal—swinging mechanism that allows a stove to stay level with horizon when the boat heels

give-way vessel—when two boats meet, the one expected to alter course and/or speed to prevent a collision

gooseneck—swivel fitting attaching the boom to mast

gust—a sudden increase in wind velocity, also called a puff

half hitch—knot used to tie line to an object

halyard—wire or line that pulls the sail up

hank—a fastener by which a sail is attached to a stay

hard alee—command of execution when tacking

hard aground—boat is stuck on the bottom

harden up—turn the boat toward the wind

harness—heavy nylon straps joined by stainless clip and tether, worn over shoulders and around waist in heavy weather

hatches—hinged doors on top of cabin

head—marine toilet; often used to refer to entire bathroom aboard

head (of sail)—the top corner of the sail

header—wind shift toward the bow

headstay—the foremost stay from bow to top of mast

headway/steerageway—forward motion, enough to steer effectively

heeling—when a sailboat leans to the lee

horseshoe life preserver—U-shaped floatable collar mounted on stern to toss overboard if someone in water needs help

hull—body of boat

hull speed—boat's theoretical maximum speed

in irons/in stays—head to wind and dead in the water

initial stability—resistance to heeling up to about 12°

jacklines—wire rigged from bow to stern along both sides of deck to clip harness tether into in heavy weather

jib—foresail carried on the jibstay

jib hanks—snaps to connect jib to stay

jib lead—adjustable fairlead for jibsheets, determines angle of jibsheet to the clew

jibe—to change tacks downwind

jibe ho—command of execution when jibing

jibsheet—line tied to clew of jib or genoa that adjusts sail in and out

jibstay—wire from bow to mast (but not to masthead)

jiffy reef—reef in the mainsail that is tied rather than rolled

kedge off—use anchor to pull boat off a shoal

keel—vertical fin under boat with weight for stability

knockdown—boat is blown over such that both mast and keel lie at waterline

knot—one nautical mile per hour

knotmeter—measures speed in knots

latitude—see **parallels of latitude**

lazarette—storage compartment usually located under cockpit seat bench

leech—the trailing edge of a sail

leech cord—small line running up inside leech to reduce flutter

lee helm—bow turns to leeward when tiller is released

leeward—in the direction opposite from which the wind is blowing (pronounced *looward*)

leeway—side-slipping to leeward

length at waterline (LWL)—distance between points where bow and stern touch the water at rest

length overall (LOA)—distance from the tip of bow to end of stern

lifelines—safety wires running the length of the deck

LifeSling—floatable device thrown to person in distress in water

lift—wind shift toward the stern

locker—storage area found under settees, behind cushions, and on deck

longitude—see **meridians of longitude**

lower shrouds—shrouds that lead from base of spreaders to deck

luff—spill wind out of a sail

luff (of a sail)—the leading edge of the sail

lull—sudden reduction in wind velocity

magnetic north—direction indicated by north-seeking magnetic compass

main—short for mainsail

main halyard—line that raises and lowers the mainsail

main saloon—living area in a cruising boat, where seats and dining table are found

mainsail—sail hoisted along after edge of mainmast (pronounced *mainsl*)

mast—vertical spar supporting sails

mast step—plate that holds bottom of mast in place

masthead—top of mast

masthead fly—device at top of mast to indicate wind direction

masthead rig—jibstay runs from top of mast to bow of boat

meridians of longitude—measures angle to east and west of Greenwich, England

messenger—light line used to feed heavier line or blocks to areas not easily reached

mooring—a permanent buoy to which one ties a boat

nav station—designated area for navigation below, usually has flat area for working on charts with storage for charts, navigation aids, and mounted electronics

neutral helm—no tug on the tiller; no weather or lee helm

no-go zone—area between close-hauled and directly into wind where boat cannot sail and is dead in the water, in irons

nun—even-numbered conical navigation buoy, usually red

outhaul—line attached to clew of sail on a boom that adjusts foot tension

overhaul—to pull the slack out of a sheet to trim a sail

overpowered—excessive heeling in comparison to forward drive

painter—tow line permanently secured at bow of dinghy

parallel ruler—draws parallel lines to transfer course or bearing on a chart

parallels of latitude—measures angle north or south of the equator

pinch—to sail too close to the wind to maintain speed

pitching—precipitous rising and falling of the bow on steep seas

planing—exceeding theoretical hull speed by skimming the water

play—to adjust trim in and out constantly

point—to sail close to the wind

point (on a compass)—one of 32 divisions of the compass (11.25°)

points of sail—close-hauled, reaching, and running; describe relationship between wind direction and boat's heading

port side—the boat's left side

port tack—sailing with the main boom on starboard side

portholes—cabin windows that can be opened

portlights—cabin windows that cannot be opened

positive stability—self-righting if turned over

prepare to jibe—command of preparation when jibing

preventer—a line tied to a boom to prevent an accidental jibe

projected area—the actual hull or sail area exposed to the water or wind

puff—a gust of wind, see **gust**

quarter—portion of the boat between the beam and the stern

quarter wave—wave following boat at angle to stern quarter

Quick Stop Method—to pick up person overboard by turning through the wind to back the jib

reach—sailing with the wind across the boat

ready about—command of preparation when tacking

reef—to shorten or reduce size of sail

reeve—to pass a line through a fitting

rigging—all the wire and rope on a boat

roach—convex area of sail lying aft of a straight line from head to clew when viewed from the side

roller-furling jib—headsail that rolls up vertically

rolling hitch—a knot that can be used to hold tension when tied to another line

rope clutches—leads for halyards with levers that act as a brake

rudder—underwater fin turned by tiller or wheel to steer the boat

rudderpost—metal tube or bar that turns the rudder, connects rudder to tiller or steering quadrant

run—sailing with the wind from behind the boat

running rigging—all lines, tackles, etc., that adjust the sails

sail ties—nylon or rope strips used to tie up mainsail when stored on boom

schooner—boat with two or more masts, with aft mast the tallest of the two

scope—relation of length of anchor line used to depth of water

scull—moving the rudder back and forth like a flipper to propel the boat

seacocks—valves that open and close the through-hull fittings

sentinel—a weight placed on anchor rode to reduce angle line makes with bottom

set—describes a sail that is raised and full of wind

settees—bench-like seats in cruising boats

sheets—lines attached to clew of sails to adjust trim

ship (water)—to take on seawater into the cockpit or dinghy

shooting—to turn directly into the wind

shrouds—wires running abeam from masthead to the deck that hold up the mast

sloop—single-masted vessel with a jib

slot effect—tendency of jib to make mainsail more effective

snub—to place one wrap around a cleat or winch to absorb much of its pull

soundings—depths on a chart in meters, fathoms, or feet

spar—general term for mast, boom, pole, etc.

spinnaker—a light parachute-like sail for sailing downwind

spinnaker pole—spar to position tack of spinnaker

spinnaker sheet—line to clew of spinnaker opposite the pole

spreader—struts that spread the angle shrouds make with the mast

spring lines—docklines that keep the boat parallel to the dock

stall—inability of wind to stay attached to lee side of sail

stand-on vessel—when two boats meet, the boat that's expected to maintain its course and speed unless risk of collision exists

standing rigging—all the fixed rigging that holds up masts (shrouds and stays)

starboard side—the boat's right side

starboard tack—sailing with the main boom on port side

stays—wires from the mast to the bow and stern that keep the mast from falling forward or aft

staysail—small jib tacked between mast and headstay

steerageway—enough speed to steer effectively

stem—forward edge of the bow

stern—extreme after end of a vessel

stern line—docking line used to hold stern of boat to dock

sump—catch area or low point in the bilge below floorboards, where water drains

surfing—sliding down the face of a wave

tabling—edging on the leech of a sail

tack—to change tacks with the bow passing through the wind

tack (of boat)—see **port tack** and **starboard tack**

tack (of sail)—forward lower corner

tail—to pull a line behind a winch

tail (of a line)—free end of a line

telltales—wool or other light strips of material placed on shrouds or sail to show wind direction or flow

tiller—arm fitted to rudderpost to steer by

topping lift—support line or wire from masthead to end of main boom, used to hold boom upright when sail is not set

topsides—the sides of the hull above the waterline; also used when describing going from below to deck

transom—the usually flat portion of the stern running across the boat

traveler—track running athwartship to change mainsail's angle

trim (fore and aft)—the attitude of the boat, bow up or bow down

trim (sail)—to pull in, to adjust the set

true north—direction to the geographical north pole

true wind—the wind as felt when stationary

turnbuckle—a fitting, adjustable in length, that attaches bottom of shrouds and stays to chainplates

ultimate stability—ability of boat to resist turning over

upper shrouds—shrouds that lead to masthead

variation—local difference in degrees between true and magnetic north

veering—wind direction shifting clockwise, such as S to SW

warp—threads that run lengthwise in sailcloth

weather helm—tendency of boat to head into the wind when helm is released

weigh anchor—to raise the anchor aboard

winch—a drum with gears and handle to assist pulling in lines under strain

windlass—electric winch mounted in deck locker in bow, used to raise anchor and chain

windward—in the direction from which the wind is blowing

wing and wing—sailing downwind with jib on one side and main on opposite side

INDEX